STAFF TRAINING AND RECOGNITION PROGRAM

BASIC ACCOUNTING
(S300)
(THIRD EDITION)

Written by Tom Ryan
2002 revisions by Keith Peterson
Produced by Jim Jerving
Editorial coordination by Rena Crispin
Center for Professional Development
CUNA & Affiliates

Copyright © 1991, 1995, 2002
Credit Union National Association, Inc.

ISBN 0-7872-9285-0

All rights reserved. No part of this publication may be reproduced, stored in a retrieval system, or transmitted, in any form or by any means, electronic, mechanical, photocopying, recording or otherwise, without the prior written permission of the copyright owner.

Printed in the United States of America

10 9 8 7 6 5 4 3 2 1

KENDALL/HUNT PUBLISHING COMPANY
4050 Westmark Drive P.O. Box 1840 Dubuque, Iowa 52004-1840

With respect to the content of this publication, neither the Credit Union National Association, Inc. (CUNA), nor any of its affiliates or its or their respective employees make any express or implied warranty or assume any legal liability or responsibility for the accuracy, completeness, or usefulness of any information, commercial product, service, process, provider, vendor, or trade name/mark that is disclosed. References to any specific commercial product, service, process, provider, vendor, or trade name/mark in this publication also does not necessarily constitute or imply that such product or provider is endorsed, recommended, or warranted by CUNA. The views and opinions of the authors expressed herein do not necessarily state or reflect those of CUNA and such reference shall not be used for advertising or product endorsement purposes.

This publication is designed to provide accurate and authoritative information in regard to the subject matter covered. It is sold with the understanding that the publisher, Credit Union National Association, Inc., is not engaged in rendering legal, accounting, or other professional services. If legal advice or other expert assistance is required, the services of a competent professional person should be sought.

Contents

Acknowledgments		iv
About the Authors		iv
Preface		vi
	Introduction	1
Chapter 1	Accounting Concepts	3
Chapter 2	Recording Transactions	19
Chapter 3	Recording Adjustments and Preparing the Trial Balance Worksheet	33
Chapter 4	Financial Statements and the Closing of Accounts	45
Chapter 5	Accounting for Fixed Assets	55
Chapter 6	Accounting for Liabilities and Equity	63
Chapter 7	Special Journals and Subsidiary Ledgers	73
Appendix A	Answers to Activities	83
Appendix B	Glossary	87
Appendix C	Resources	91
Appendix D	Test Questions	99
Index		107

Acknowledgments

CUNA & Affiliates, Inc. expresses special thanks to the following individuals for their valuable suggestions and comments:

- Gail DeBoer, SAC Federal Credit Union
- Robert S. Korthase, CCUE, CFP, 66 Federal Credit Union
- Joyce Harris (formerly with Heartland Credit Union)
- Maria Knickmeier, CUNA & Affiliates, Inc.

About the Authors

Keith Peterson is chief financial officer for CUNA Credit Union in Madison, Wisconsin. Before coming to the credit union in 1998, he served as vice president of economics and statistics at CUNA & Affiliates. He earned a bachelor's degree in economics from Iowa State University and a Master of Science degree in economics from the University of Wisconsin-Madison. He holds the Chartered Financial Analyst designation and has contributed to a number of credit union publications covering financial management, accounting, and economics.

Thomas J. Ryan is a certified public accountant and former lead accounting instructor at Madison Area Technical College in Madison, Wisconsin. He has been named the Outstanding Teacher of the Year by the student senate.

The **Staff Training and Recognition (STAR)** program is designed to benefit all credit union staff members. The STAR program is divided into separate learning tracks. To be eligible for a STAR certificate and lapel pin, you must successfully complete all courses in the learning track you have chosen to pursue.

Basic Accounting

The Staff Training and Recognition (STAR) Program

Core Courses Required for All Tracks	
S010 Credit Union Orientation S020 Member Relations S030 Security	
Tracks	**Track Courses**
Member Services	S100 Money and Negotiable Instruments S110 Member Services S120 Cross-Selling
Consumer Lending	S200 The Lending Process S210 Lending Products and Regulations S220 Collections
Credit Union Accounting	S300 Basic Accounting S310 Accounting for Credit Unions S320 Credit Union Financial Analysis
Advanced Lending	S400 Bankruptcy and Court Proceedings S410 Mortgage Lending S420 Loan Marketing
Credit Union Sales	S500 Improving and Maintaining Quality Service S510 Successful Sales Techniques S520 Interpersonal Skills: Understanding Your Impact on Members
Credit Union Technology	S600 Credit Union Technology S610 Working with Technology S620 Serving Members with Technology
Loan Officer	S700 Loan Interviewing S710 Loan Underwriting S720 Loan Servicing
Savings Plus	S800 Opening New Accounts S810 Individual Retirement Accounts S820 Investment Choices for Members
Credit Union Security	S900 Preventing Fraud S910 Security Issues
Professional and Career Development	S1000 Develop a Career Plan: Practical Tools and Methods for Mapping Your Career S1010 Write Effectively: Credit Union Business Writing Techniques S1020 Make Work Manageable: Time, Stress, and Workload Management Strategies
Member Services Level II	S1100 Working Effectively with Difficult Members and Staff S1110 Helping Members Understand and Solve Problems: Your Role as Financial Educator S1120 Using Technology to Improve Member Service
Financial Management	S1200 Financial Management Made Easy I: Financial Statements and Budgeting S1210 Financial Management Made Easy II: Sources and Uses of Money
Electives	S1300 Member Service: Exceeding Expectations S1310 Successful Collections: Balancing Member Service and Credit Union Interests S1320 Robbery Prevention and Preparation

Preface

About These Courses

The STAR courses are not intended to provide legal advice, and we do not guarantee the information is appropriate for all state-chartered credit unions. If you have any legal or policy questions, contact your credit union president or your credit union league.

How to Use This Course

If you are sight-impaired and choose to have this course read to you, we suggest that a spouse, partner, friend, or volunteer from your credit union or credit union league assist you. You can also check with your local library regarding reader services available in your community.

If you are participating in a seminar, your instructor will get you started.

If you are completing this course through correspondence study, please follow this procedure:
1. Read the chapter opening objectives to get an idea of what's ahead.
2. Read the text. Complete the activities as you read each chapter. (Answers for many of the activities are included in the appendices.)
3. When you have read the text and completed the activities, take the competency test.

Competency Test Instructions

Each course in the STAR program has a competency test of forty multiple choice questions. To successfully complete the course, you must correctly answer at least thirty-two questions. You can refer to the text as you take the test, but the test must be completed individually.

If you are participating in a seminar, your instructor will provide directions. If you are completing this course through correspondence study, please follow this procedure:
1. Locate the test questions in the last appendix of the text.
2. Find a quiet place where you can work undisturbed and at your own pace.
3. Record your answers on the answer sheet that was mailed to you along with the text. Follow the instructions on this sheet for marking answers.
4. Complete the identification section on the answer sheet and make sure you have marked an answer for each question.
5. Mail the scannable answer sheets to CUNA's National Processing Center in the envelope provided. Mail competency test answer sheets to your league education department.

Introduction

Basic Accounting is the first in a series of three courses in the Accounting track of the STAR program. You will be introduced to the terminology and the mechanics of the recordkeeping function of accounting. The recordkeeping function of accounting is called bookkeeping. Though you'll see many credit union examples used to illustrate recordkeeping principles, the purpose of this course is to introduce concepts that apply to many different kinds of businesses, not just to credit unions.

Bookkeeping includes the study of a double-entry system where there are at least two components to every transaction. Thus, when a piece of equipment is purchased for cash, the bookkeeper records not only the decrease in cash but also the increase in the amount of equipment owned. To record transactions efficiently, accountants have developed a set of journals and ledgers to be used in the recording function. This first course in basic accounting introduces you to the use of journals and ledgers to record and store financial information.

The second course in this series, *Accounting for Credit Unions* builds on this introduction. Once you understand the basics of accounting, you'll be able to apply that understanding to the unique features of accounting for credit unions. The final course in the accounting track is *Credit Union Financial Analysis*. This course provides the tools you need to use the information the accounting system provides to make good business decisions.

As you can see, the three courses in this track build on one another. It is, therefore, extremely important that you begin this sequence with a solid foundation. As you study basic accounting, keep a pencil, notepad, and calculator handy to record key ideas and verify dollar amounts. The more active you become in your study of accounting, the more in-depth your understanding will be.

Chapter 1 Accounting Concepts

Accounting is the process of recording and interpreting financial information for a business or organization. Every single transaction is documented—broken down into individual components, recorded, transferred, totaled, and included on financial statements. There's a wealth of detail involved, there are specific rules to follow, and finding a mistake can be like trying to find the proverbial needle in the haystack. But reliable, timely financial information is essential to the long-term success of any business or other organization.

Accounting Is a Decision-Making Tool

Most people who look at the data produced by an accounting system use the information to make choices of one kind or another. The major users of this information include:

- *People who run organizations.* Accounting provides essential information about financial resources and their uses so that managers and boards of directors can measure progress toward goals, observe the outcomes of past decisions, make sound decisions on how to run their organizations in the future, identify problems, and more. They use financial information to shape a better organization and to ensure a long-term operation.

- *People who own organizations.* When a business has many owners, a board of directors is usually elected to oversee operations on their behalf. The directors are accountable to the people who elected them; they provide an annual report on operations that includes the financial results. Owners, including credit union members, use that financial information to evaluate the

Objectives

> Upon completion of this chapter, you will be able to
> 1. name the major users of accounting information;
> 2. identify the different types of business organizations;
> 3. prepare a simple income statement and balance sheet;
> 4. understand the effects of transactions on the balance sheet equation;
> 5. explain how the balance sheet and income statement are related.

Reliable, timely financial information is essential to the long-term success of any business or other organization.

ACCOUNTING CONCEPTS

success and stability of the organization in which they have a stake. They may decide to increase or decrease their investment accordingly. The organization's financial stability and success (or lack of it) may influence who the owners elect to represent them on the board. Potential owners may also consider financial information before investing in an organization.

- *Government agencies.* Local, state, and federal governments require accounting information to assess correct taxes. In the financial industry, regulatory agencies require accounting and other information to evaluate the safety and soundness of each institution, especially those covered by government-backed deposit insurance funds.

- *Creditors.* Before people decide to extend credit to a business or organization, either as a loan or as approval to buy on credit, they usually evaluate financial information to assess the amount of risk involved. Even though your credit union is in the business of lending money to members, it may need to borrow money or buy on credit to purchase property, equipment, or supplies, or to cover a short-term cash-flow need.

Characteristics of Accounting Information

Given the ways financial information is used, the accounting process should have several characteristics to make it useful for the people who rely on the data.

Information needs to be accurate. Incorrect information leads to poor decisions.

Reports should provide the optimal amount of information. Too much can be as useless as too little. Different groups are often given different amounts of detail, according to their needs.

Information has to be understood by many different people. To make this easier, organizations usually follow a set of recommended rules, statements, and formats known as generally accepted accounting principles (GAAP).

Information must be timely, especially for management decision making. Generally, the longer an undesirable situation continues, the more damage is done, and the harder it becomes to correct. Opportunities may also be missed without timely data.

Finally, accounting information should be consistent; results from different periods can be compared to show trends in the business. Using generally accepted accounting principles helps provide consistency. This is not to say accounting procedures should never change. Both generally accepted accounting principles and regulatory requirements shift over time. Changes should generally be made for the purpose of providing more accurate or more useful information on the true financial position of an organization. Except for these occasional changes, however, the same methods and calculations should be used year after year.

Accounting and Bookkeeping

The accounting function has two major components. The first could be considered the management portion of the function. This component includes analyzing the types of transactions a business will have and deciding how these transactions should be measured or valued, when they should be recognized, and how they should be reported in the financial statements—in other words, setting up the financial recordkeeping system that will be used by an organization. Procedural decisions are usually made by a professional accountant who also determines when and what types of changes to the system are appropriate. He or she may analyze the financial statements in some detail to provide additional information on an organization's current status.

The second component of the accounting function is operating the system after it's been designed. The actual recordkeeping and preparation of financial statements is usually handled by a bookkeeper following the practices and procedures set forth by the accountant.

This course provides the background to do the basics of the bookkeeping function.

Overview of the Bookkeeping Process

Each organization must decide how often to summarize and review its financial situation. Most organizations need annual results for owners, creditors, and/or government agencies. But management needs information more often than once a year. So, most organizations also prepare reports on a quarterly or monthly basis. The amount of time covered by a financial report is known as an accounting period.

You'll probably be using a computer-based accounting system in your credit union work, but we've chosen to introduce the bookkeeping process using a manual accounting system. The reason is simple. Computer systems are based on manual

---

The amount of time covered by a financial report is known as an accounting period.

ACCOUNTING CONCEPTS

systems. If you understand the mechanics of a manual system, the computer accounting system will hold no mysteries for you.

A simplified version of the basic bookkeeping process for a manual accounting system is presented in figure 1.1 and briefly described here.

1. *Analyze and record each transaction in a journal.* Transactions are recorded in chronological order in a record book called a journal. For each transaction, the bookkeeper notes which financial categories, or accounts, should be changed as a result of the transaction. Most businesses, including credit unions, use the double-entry system of bookkeeping, so each transaction affects at least two accounts. Double-entry bookkeeping and journals are introduced in chapter 2.

2. *Post transactions to a ledger.* After a transaction is recorded in a journal, the changes to the various accounts are transferred, or posted, to a ledger. While a page in a journal may note every transaction in a single day, a page in a ledger records all the changes in a single account. The ledger is introduced in chapter 2.

3. *Prepare a trial balance.* At the end of a period, the bookkeeper prepares to close the books by checking for obvious mistakes. Since double-entry bookkeeping records transactions as matching increases and/or decreases (debits and credits), a trial balance compares the total debit and credit balances of the organization's accounts to be sure they are equal. Debits, credits, and the trial balance are also discussed in more detail in chapter 2.

4. *Prepare adjustments.* At the end of any accounting period, most businesses need to record certain types of financial transactions not covered elsewhere in the books. For example, a business incurs an obligation for property taxes during each month, even though the tax is only paid once a year. Interest is earned on a savings account every month, even if it is only received once a quarter. The accounting entries that recognize these otherwise unrecorded transactions are called adjusting entries; they adjust the books to accurately reflect all income and expenses associated with the period. Adjustments are listed on a worksheet and checked for accuracy. They are not recorded until after the financial statements have been prepared (see chapter 3).

5. *Prepare financial statements.* Statements that summarize financial information about a business are prepared from the worksheet. These summary statements are a key product of the accounting system. They convey the information managers, boards, owners, and others need to be able to make various types of decisions. Financial statements are introduced later in this chapter.

Basic Accounting
ACCOUNTING CONCEPTS

Figure 1.1 Overview of the Bookkeeping Process

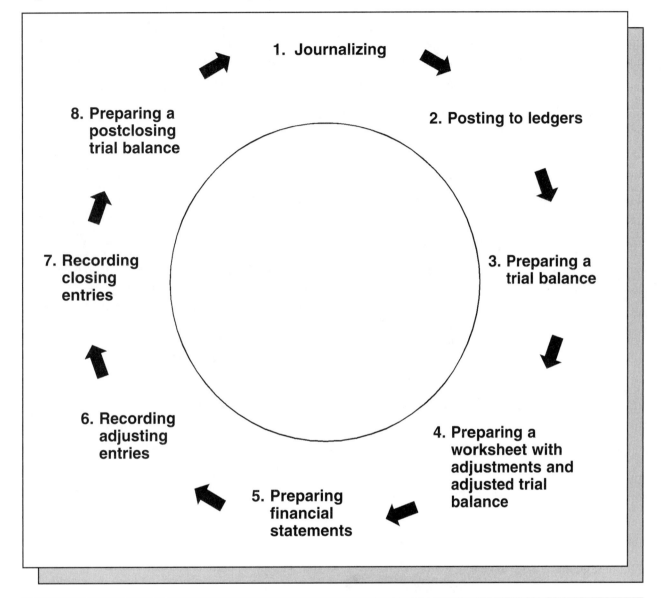

6. *Record adjusting entries.* The adjusting entries are journalized and posted to bring the books up-to-date for the period.

7. *Close the books.* Before recording any transactions from a new accounting period, certain accounts must be reduced to a zero balance. This process is known as closing the books. It is discussed in chapter 4.

8. *Prepare a postclosing trial balance.* Another trial balance at this final stage provides a check on the accuracy of adjusting and closing entries. The postclosing trial balance is covered in chapter 4.

ACCOUNTING CONCEPTS

Although it would seem logical to introduce bookkeeping in a sequence that follows a transaction from its initiation to its final summary in a financial statement, the process is actually easier to comprehend if we look at the end product first, so you understand where you're going. Once you grasp the accounting concepts financial statements are based on, and once you see how individual transactions are organized into useful information, you'll find it easier to follow the process of analyzing and recording financial data.

First, however, you need to know how private businesses are organized under the law, because the type of business organization affects some aspects of the accounting process.

Test your understanding of the bookkeeping process. Complete activity 1.1.

Types of Business Organizations

The three most common forms of business organizations—aside from governmental organizations—are

1. sole proprietorship;
2. partnership;
3. corporation.

Each of these forms is characterized by a unique combination of ownership, control structure, and legal status.

A **sole proprietorship** is a business owned by a single individual. That individual invests the money to get the business up and running. He or she has the authority to make all decisions about the business and how it will be run. In a legal sense, the owner and the business are inseparable. Profits of the business are income for the owner. The owner is personally responsible for all obligations or liabilities of the business.

A **partnership** is very similar to a sole proprietorship, except that it has more than one owner. Ownership, however, does not have to be on an equal basis. Each person's share of responsibilities, liabilities, and profits is usually specified in a carefully prepared partnership agreement.

Corporations are legal entities created by law. They are usually chartered or incorporated under state law, generally in the state where the principal office is located. One of the most important advantages incorporation offers a business is that its owners have limited legal liability. If the business has a loss or goes bankrupt, individual owners may lose their investment in the corporation, but they aren't personally responsible for any of its debts. Owners exercise control of the corporation by electing a board of directors to oversee operations and to make policy decisions.

Most people think of corporations as being owned by people who purchase shares of stock in the hope of earning a return through dividends (distributions of profits) or through an increase in the value of the stock. This describes many investor-owned, for-profit corporations, but there are also special types of corporations, including cooperative corporations, not-for-profit

Basic Accounting
ACCOUNTING CONCEPTS

Activity 1.1 Understanding the Bookkeeping Process

Match the steps of the bookkeeping process in the first column with the definitions in the second column.

____ 1. Journalizing

____ 2. Posting

____ 3. Preparing a trial balance

____ 4. Preparing financial statements

____ 5. Recording adjusting entries

____ 6. Recording closing entries

____ 7. Preparing postclosing trial balance

____ a. Transferring transactions to appropriate accounts

____ b. Recording transactions in the journal and ledger that are not covered elsewhere

____ c. Recording transactions as they occur throughout the accounting period

____ d. Checking the accuracy of adjusting and closing entries

____ e. Conveying financial information to various individuals to make decisions

____ f. Reducing certain accounts to a zero balance

____ g. Comparing total debit and credit balances in all accounts to be sure they are equal

Answers appear in appendix A.

---

charitable corporations, and others. Credit unions are not-for-profit cooperative corporations chartered and operated under the Federal Credit Union Act or similar state laws.

Recordkeeping for the various types of business organizations is similar in many ways. Differences in terminology occur, but the main difference is in the way the owners' financial interest in the business is handled. We'll look at this difference at the appropriate point in our discussion of financial statements.

Summarize your understanding of the three types of businesses in activity 1.2.

Financial Statements

As we stated earlier, financial statements are summaries that convey key information to management, boards, owners, and others. Each business needs slightly different information, so each business prepares a set of reports that meets its individual needs.

Basic Accounting

ACCOUNTING CONCEPTS

Activity 1.2 Describing the Types of Businesses

List the differences between the three most common types of businesses: sole proprietorship, partnership, and corporation.

_____
_____
_____
_____
_____
_____
_____
_____
_____

What type of business is your credit union? _____

Despite the individual differences, however, everyone with an interest in a business's financial success wants to know if it's earning more than it is spending and what its overall financial condition is. The income statement and balance sheet answer these questions. They are the two fundamental financial reports for all businesses. Every financial transaction is reflected on one or both of these statements. Accounting systems are organized around them, so when you analyze transactions, you'll be organizing them by how they will affect these two statements.

The income statement and balance sheet each follow an overall format established by generally accepted accounting principles. General categories of accounts and organizing principles are the same regardless of the type of business. However, the specific accounts listed in each category often change according to the nature of the business. For instance, interest on loans is an important income account for a credit union but not for a retail firm. Even within a firm, the number of accounts listed on a statement may depend on the needs of the intended readers. Though both the balance sheet and income statement are summaries,

> Everyone with an interest in a business's financial success wants to know if it's earning more than it is spending.

copies intended for management are likely to include more detail than copies intended for others. When you record financial transactions, you will enter them at the most detailed level of information your accounting system is set up to provide.

The Income Statement

The **income statement** is perhaps the most important financial statement of a company or credit union. It shows whether the business has earned a net financial gain during a specific period of time. It helps the board and staff manage the flow of money into and out of the business. The income statement shows two major types of accounts—income and expenses. Figure 1.2 shows a simple income statement for a sole proprietor. (*Note:* According to accounting convention, a single underscore indicates the items above the line are to be added. The total is shown with a double underline.)

Income is the amount of cash or receivables a business gains as a result of its operation. A receivable is a debt owed to the business that will be paid within a relatively short period of time. For many businesses, income is generated by the sale of goods or services to customers and earnings on investments. Most credit union income is derived from interest earned on loans and investments, plus fees charged for services. John Nelson's business (figure 1.2) had income totaling $75,000. Note that the income is broken down by the types of services Nelson provides. Income from each of these services is recorded in a separate account.

Expenses are the costs of goods or services acquired or consumed in the operation of the business. John Nelson acquired services from employees (salaries expense) and consumed office supplies and other expenses that total $26,260. Five accounts are shown under expenses in this simple example. Credit unions' main expenses are dividends, salaries, benefits, office occupancy, and office operation. Many other types of expenses occur as well.

Figure 1.2 Income Statement

John Nelson, CPA
Income Statement
For the Year Ended December 31, 20XX

Income:

Monthly write-up of financial statements	$20,000	
Tax return preparation	30,000	
Audit fees	25,000	
Total income		$75,000

Operating Expenses:

Salaries expense	18,000	
Rent expense	6,000	
Utilities expense	1,000	
Telephone expense	760	
Office supplies expense	500	
Total operating expenses		26,260
Net income		$48,740

ACCOUNTING CONCEPTS

The difference between total income and total expenses for the period covered by the statement is known as **net income.** In figure 1.2, for example, the $48,740 is the net income for the twelve-month period ending December 31, 20XX. Although this example covers a year, any period of time can be used. Credit unions generally prepare financial statements for each month and for the full year.

The Balance Sheet

The **balance sheet** is the statement that shows the financial condition of a business on a particular date. It is sometimes called a **statement of financial condition** (figure 1.3). It shows the value of everything the business owns, what it owes, and the value of the owners' interest. One of the balance sheet's most important uses is assessing the overall strength of the business. Unlike the income statement, which includes only events that take place during the period covered, the balance sheet shows the cumulative effects of all financial transactions, from the day the business began through the date of the statement. The balance sheet has three major types of accounts—**assets, liabilities,** and **equity.** Figure 1.4 shows the balance sheet of another sole proprietorship.

Asset accounts show items of value whose worth can be established in monetary terms. They are the resources owned or effectively controlled by the business. Examples include cash, receivables, merchandise inventory, supplies, equipment, buildings, and land. The balance sheet of Carol O'Brien's law firm (figure 1.4) shows four asset accounts with a total value of $11,500 as of December 31, 20XX.

Liabilities are the debts and obligations owed to others as a result of past events. Examples of **liability accounts** are accounts payable, wages payable, taxes payable, notes payable, and mortgages payable. The attorney in figure 1.4 has only one type of liability—accounts payable—totaling $1,500.

Equity accounts represent the value of the owners' stake in the business. That stake is equal to the share of total assets not offset by creditors' claims. Creditors' claims always take precedence over those of owners, so *equity equals total assets minus total liabilities.* The accounts used in the equity section of the balance sheet vary with the type of business organization.

Figure 1.3 Differences in Terminology

Differences in Terminology

Different types of businesses use different words to refer to certain items on financial statements. Sometimes the difference results from a for-profit versus a not-for-profit orientation. In other cases, the reason for using one word rather than another is less clear.

The left column below presents terms most often used by credit unions. These are the terms we use in this module. On the right you'll see other terms that may be used for the same or similar items.

Income statement	**Profit and loss statement**
Income	**Revenue**
Net income	**Profit, surplus, or margin**
Balance sheet	**Statement of financial condition**
Equity	**Capital**
Undivided earnings	**Retained earnings**

Figure 1.4 Balance Sheet

Carol O'Brien, Attorney
Balance Sheet
December 31, 20XX

Assets		Liabilities	
Cash	$8,000	Accounts payable	$1,500
Office supplies	500	**Equity**	
Prepaid insurance	1,000		
Office furniture and equipment	2,000	Carol O'Brien, capital	10,000
Total assets	$11,500	Total liabilities and equity	$11,500

A sole proprietorship has one equity account, called a capital account. Figure 1.4 shows $10,000 as the value of Carol O'Brien's interest in her business. That value will change as the net effect of sales and purchases shifts the amounts of assets and liabilities.

Tracking the equity in a partnership can become very complex since it must follow the specifications of the partnership agreement. In their simplest form, however, the accounting entries for each partner's equity will look like those made for a sole proprietor. Changes in assets and liabilities will increase or decrease each partner's capital account according to the partnership agreement.

The equity of an investor-owned corporation, at a minimum, includes accounts for common stock and retained earnings. The common stock account reflects what investors paid for the original issue of the shares of common stock. The retained earnings account reflects the cumulative net income of the corporation that has not been paid out to the stockholders.

Credit unions have a unique situation in regard to equity. Members are the owners of a credit union, and their savings deposits—their shares—are their ownership equity in the organization. However, the American Institute of Certified Public Accountants (AICPA), one of the groups that help shape generally accepted accounting principles, believes that shares should be treated as liabilities, in the same manner that banks treat their customers' deposits. To resolve this issue, the National Credit Union Administration (NCUA) approved recording member shares as a separate category on the balance sheet, between liabilities and equity. In this course, we record shares using the NCUA method.

Basic Accounting
ACCOUNTING CONCEPTS

Aside from member shares, a credit union has two types of equity accounts—regular reserves and undivided earnings. **Regular reserves** are earnings used to protect the credit union from losses such as loan defaults. They are not available for distribution as dividends. **Undivided earnings** are aggregate earnings of the credit union throughout its operation that have not been transferred to regular reserves.

Although the balance sheet and income statement answer different questions about a business's financial status, they are related. Common sense will tell you that all income and expenses—the items shown on the income statement—affect an organization's financial condition, which is shown on the balance sheet. In the next section, we trace the effect of individual transactions on a balance sheet. But when you're looking at the cumulative effects of a month's or a year's worth of transactions, you'll usually only see a direct connection between the two statements in one portion of each report; the amount of net income from the income statement equals the change that took place over the period in the balance sheet's undivided earnings account. The mechanics for adding a period's net income to the undivided earnings balance are described in chapter 4.

Review the various types of accounts shown on financial statements by completing activity 1.3.

Activity 1.3 Reviewing Financial Statements

Read through the following list of accounts and note whether each is found on the income statement (I) or balance sheet (B).

_B_   1. Accounts receivable
_B_   2. Member shares
_I_   3. Salaries
_B_   4. Office equipment
_I_   5. Rent
_I_   6. Earnings on investments
_B_   7. Loans payable
_I_   8. Service fees
_B_   9. Taxes payable
_B_ 10. Regular reserves

Answers appear in appendix A.

The Balance Sheet Equation

You have probably noticed that both columns in the sample balance sheet (figure 1.4) add up to the same dollar total. All balance sheets work this way. The business's financial condition is shown as the dollar value of its resources and the dollar value of the claims against the business by creditors and owners. Because the owners' claim (equity) equals the difference between the value of the assets and the creditors' claims, the two sides of the balance sheet are always equal. This idea is expressed in the balance sheet equation:

Assets = Liabilities + Equity

A credit union that leaves member shares unclassified would write the equation this way:

Assets = Liabilities + Shares + Equity

A transaction that is analyzed and recorded correctly always maintains this balance. Thus, every transaction must be recorded at least twice, because a change in any area of the equation must be offset by another change (or changes) of an equal amount. Let's look at a series of transactions to illustrate this. (*Note:* the method we use to show transactions in this chapter is not the method used by a business to keep its books. The method shown here is only a convenience to help you visualize how transactions affect the balance sheet equation. The method for recording transactions in an accounting system is introduced in chapter 2.)

> Because the owners' claim (equity) equals the difference between the value of the assets and the creditors' claims, the two sides of the balance sheet are always equal.

On October 1, employees of Royal Manufacturing pooled their savings to establish the Royal Credit Union. Members deposited $10,000, which was recorded as a cash asset and as shares. This transaction shows matching increases on both sides of the balance sheet equation:

Assets = Liabilities + Shares + Equity

	Cash		Shares
(1)	10,000	=	10,000

The board decided to invest $9,000 in U.S. government securities so the credit union could earn income. A new asset account appeared on the balance sheet—investments. What offset that asset increase? A decrease in the cash account by the amount used to pay for the investments.

Assets = Liabilities + Shares + Equity

	Cash		Investments		Shares
(1)	10,000				10,000
(2)	−9,000		+9,000		
	1,000	+	9,000	=	10,000

In this transaction, both changes were made on the same side of the equation, but since the two asset accounts had an equal amount of increases and decreases, total assets remained unchanged and the equation remained balanced.

A little later, the credit union purchased a personal computer and printer, paying $500 down and signing a note for the remaining

ACCOUNTING CONCEPTS

$3,500. In this transaction, the increase in assets due to the computer system was offset by two other changes—a liability that didn't exist previously, and a reduction in cash assets.

The net change on each side of the equation is an increase in the total of $3,500.

Now look at how income and expenses connect the balance sheet and income statement.

The credit union received a $900 interest payment on its investments. One portion of the dual entry is an increase in the asset (cash). The matching accounting entry will be recorded in an income account, not a balance sheet account. But the $900 increase in cash results in another balance sheet change. No other assets or liabilities changed as a result of the transaction. Therefore, the value of the equity increased by $900. (Remember, equity equals assets minus liabilities.) Since shares remained unchanged, the result is considered undivided earnings.

The credit union was offered subsidized office space at Royal Manufacturing and wrote a $100 check for the first month's rent. Like the income in the last example, this transaction affects both a balance sheet asset account (cash) and an income statement account (rent expense). No other asset or liability accounts are affected, and shares are unchanged. So once again, the value of the undivided earnings changes as a result of the change in assets.

Assets = Liabilities + Shares + Equity

	Cash	Investments	Equipment	Liabilities	Shares
(1)	10,000				10,000
(2)	−9,000	+9,000			
	1,000	9,000			10,000
(3)	−500		+4,000	+3,500	
	500 +	9,000 +	4,000 =	3,500 +	10,000

Assets = Liabilities + Shares + Equity

	Cash	Investments	Equipment	Liabilities	Shares	Undivided Earnings
(1)	10,000				10,000	
(2)	−9,000	+9,000				
	1,000	9,000			10,000	
(3)	−500		+4,000	+3,500		
	500	9,000	4,000	3,500	10,000	
(4)	+900					+900
	1,400 +	9,000 +	4,000 =	3,500 +	10,000 +	900

Basic Accounting
ACCOUNTING CONCEPTS

Assets = Liabilities + Shares + Equity

	Cash	Investments	Equipment	Liabilities	Shares	Undivided Earnings
(1)	10,000				10,000	
(2)	−9,000	+9,000				
	1,000	9,000			10,000	
(3)	−500		+4,000	+3,500		
	500	9,000	4,000	3,500	10,000	
(4)	+900					+900
	1,400	9,000	4,000	3,500	10,000	900
(5)	−100					−100
	1,300 +	9,000 +	4,000 =	3,500 +	10,000 +	800

Royal Credit Union's income statement for the period covered by these transactions is shown next. As you can see, the net income equals the change in undivided earnings for the period. Another way to state this is that *income increases the value of undivided earnings, while expenses decrease the value.*

Income:
Interest income $900

Expenses:
Rent expense   100

Net Income $800

In the actual recordkeeping of a business, the effect of individual income and expense transactions is not recorded directly into the undivided earnings account. Instead, the net effect of all income and expense transactions for a period—the net income—is recorded with a single entry during the closing process.

Double-Entry Accounting

The need to maintain the balance sheet equation is the basis for the double-entry accounting system used by most businesses, including credit unions. As long as the two halves of the balance sheet remain equal at the end of an accounting period, you have some assurance entries are being made properly.

You may find the double-entry system easier to comprehend and use if you remember each financial transaction represents an exchange. Something of value—usually money or the promise of money—is traded for goods, services, or a claim on the

> The need to maintain the balance sheet equation is the basis for the double-entry accounting system used by most businesses, including credit unions.

Basic Accounting
ACCOUNTING CONCEPTS

business. When you analyze a transaction, you must decide which accounts are affected by each portion of the exchange. When you record that information, you'll organize it in a format that matches the financial statements.

As you can see, the purpose of the accounting function is to provide a usable amount of accurate financial information to various groups that have an interest in a business or organization. The recording of financial information follows a logical, step-by-step process. The income statement shows the net income for a specific period of time. The balance sheet summarizes the financial condition of the business on a specific date. The equation on which the balance sheet is based is assets equal liabilities plus equity. Each transaction must be recorded as a paired set of entries. This is the basis for the double-entry bookkeeping system, which is examined in more detail in the next chapter.

Chapter 2 Recording Transactions

When a financial transaction takes place, it is documented by some type of written record—sales slip and deposit slip. In a manual accounting system, these source documents tell the accountant what transactions have taken place and must be recorded on the books.

Entry Is First Made in a Journal

Businesses normally have hundreds or even thousands of transactions in an accounting period. Journals are used to initially record every transaction, so they are known as books of original entry.

Different organizations use many different journals. The simplest and most flexible is the general journal, so we will use it to introduce the concept of journals. Later, in chapter 7, we'll look at the ways specialized journals can make recordkeeping more efficient. (Credit unions use a special journal called a journal and cash record, which is explained in detail in the *Accounting for Credit Unions* course.)

A general journal is a chronological diary of all transactions. For each transaction, space is provided to record

- the date the transaction occurred;

> *Objectives*
>
> **Upon completion of this chapter, you will be able to**
>
> 1. understand the system of double-entry accounting in which equal debits and credits are used;
> 2. analyze transactions to determine the correct debits and credits to record;
> 3. determine the normal balance (debit or credit) of any general ledger account;
> 4. record transactions in a general journal, post to a general ledger, and prepare a trial balance.

- the names of all accounts affected by the transaction;
- an explanation of the transaction;
- a reference to where the transaction was posted to the general ledger (P/R—posting reference);
- the matching debit and credit amounts.

Figure 2.1 illustrates a transaction recorded in the general journal. In the example shown, the business exchanged its promise to pay $2,000 plus interest in the future—a liability in the *notes payable* account—for two

---

A general journal is a chronological diary of all transactions.

Basic Accounting

RECORDING TRANSACTIONS

Figure 2.1 General Journal

				Page 1
Date	Account Titles and Explanation	P/R	Debit	Credit
20XX Jan. 1	Office furniture		$2000	
	Notes payable			2,000
	Purchased two desks and chairs on credit from Executive Furniture Co.			

desks and chairs worth $2,000—assets in the *office furniture* account. Only the notes payable and office furniture accounts are affected, so you see one debit and one credit in equal amounts. (Determining whether an account should be debited or credited is discussed in the next section.)

Note the format of the journal entry. The column for debits is to the left of the column for credits. This is a standard accounting format. In fact, the terms come from Latin words that originally meant *left* (**debit**) and *right* (**credit**). The name of the account to be credited—*notes payable* in this example—is indented. It's common practice to list the debit(s) first, and then indent and record the credit(s). You'll also notice that the *posting reference (P/R)* column is blank. This means the transaction hasn't been posted to the general ledger yet. At the time the transaction is transferred to the ledger, the account numbers will be recorded in the journal P/R column. (Each account is assigned an identifying number as well as a name.)

When you record transactions on the books, you enter equal amounts of debits and credits. The convention for recording them is structured in such a way that the balance sheet equation will be maintained when debits and credits match. Debit may be abbreviated *Dr;* credit may be abbreviated *Cr.*

Debits and Credits

Debits and credits are increases and decreases. If you have recordkeeping or accounting responsibility, learning how to work with debits and credits is fundamental. It's also very confusing at first because in common usage a credit is an increase and a debit is a decrease. *This is not always true in accounting.* In the special context of accounting, credits and debits

20

can be either increases or decreases, depending on the type of account under consideration.

To *increase* an account balance
- debit assets or expenses;
- credit liabilities, equity, or income.

To *decrease* an account balance
- credit assets or expenses;
- debit liabilities, equity, or income.

After working in accounting for awhile, remembering whether a given entry should be a debit or credit becomes second nature. Until then, one way to figure this out is to think through simple transactions, remembering the single principle that *debits increase assets*. Here are examples of how this leads to the other debits and credits:

- A customer pays your business cash for two hours of consulting services. Cash is an asset, so the *increased cash is a debit;* the *revenue you earned must be a credit* to balance the debits and credits.

- Your business pays cash for its monthly electricity bill. The *decrease in cash is a credit* (since debits increase assets), so the utilities *expense is a debit.*

- Your business owns a building that carries a $100,000 value in your accounts. You sell the building for $100,000. The *increased cash is a debit*, so *it must be a credit to reduce other assets* (the building).

In the special context of accounting, credits and debits can be either increases or decreases, depending on the type of account under consideration.

- Your business borrows $2,000 cash, agreeing to repay the loan plus interest in one year. The *increased cash is a debit,* so *it must be a credit to increase a liability* to record the borrowed funds.

- Your business pays an outstanding bill for office supplies. The amount owed was an accounts payable liability. *Reducing your cash balance is a credit,* so *decreasing a liability must be a debit.*

(*Note:* Credit union shares are debited and credited in the same manner as liabilities and equity: credits for increases and debits for decreases.)

Review the transactions given in chapter 1 for Royal Credit Union to determine whether the account changes should have been debits or credits. This time we'll use a standard accounting format known as a T account, which shows debits in the left column and credits in the right. The account name is given above the top bar of the T. For now, we won't concern ourselves with the balance in each account, only with the correct notation of debits and credits. (T accounts are simply a convenient way to show the entries in a single account. Transactions are not recorded this way on the books.)

Basic Accounting

RECORDING TRANSACTIONS

1. *Members deposited $10,000 in their share accounts.* They exchanged cash for a claim on the credit union. Cash is an asset. Therefore, to increase the balance in the cash account, it must be debited. To increase shares by the same amount, the account must be credited.

Cash		Member Shares	
10,000			10,000

2. *The credit union invested $9,000 in U.S. government obligations.* It exchanged cash for this investment. To decrease the cash account, the $9,000 must be recorded as a credit. Like cash, the government obligations are an asset, so the balance in the investment account is increased with a debit.

Cash		Investments	
10,000	9,000	9,000	

3. *A little later, the credit union purchased a personal computer and printer, paying $500 down and signing a note for the remaining $3,500.* It exchanged cash and a note payable for an asset. To correctly record the decrease in cash, which is an asset, the account must be credited. To increase the notes payable account, which is a liability, the $3,500 must be recorded as a credit. Finally, the furniture and equipment account must be increased from $0 to $4,000. Because the computer system is an asset, the account should be debited to increase the balance.

Cash		Notes Payable	
10,000	9,000		3,500
	500		

Furniture and Equipment	
4,000	

4. *Royal Credit Union received a $900 interest payment on its investment.* There's an income account for investment income. Income accounts are credited to increase the balance. Cash should also be increased by $900. Since cash is an asset, however, this account should be debited.

Cash		Investment Income	
10,000	9,000		900
900	500		

5. *The credit union paid $100 for a month's rent.* The credit union doesn't own the office; it is not an asset. The rent is an expense. To increase the amount shown in the account, it must be debited. Cash must be credited to record the decrease.

Cash		Rent	
10,000	9,000	100	
900	500		
	100		

Note that even though every transaction has one or more credits and one or more debits, *not* every transaction involves an increase and a decrease. In the fourth transaction, the debit and credit were both increases.

Figure 2.2 summarizes the rules for recording debits and credits and provides examples of the ways common credit union transactions are recorded.

Figure 2.3 shows the journal entries for the five Royal Credit Union transactions.

Figure 2.2 Debits/Credits and Transactions by Type of Account

Assets		Liabilities		Equity	
Debits = increases	Credits = reductions	Debits = reductions	Credits = increases	Debits = reductions	Credits = increases
Cash received, issuance of loan to member, purchase of fixed asset	Cash disbursed, sale of investment, receipt of loan principal from member	Payment of accounts unpaid from previous period, reduction of balance on outstanding debt	Purchases on credit, borrowing from Corporate Central	Net loss from income statement	Net income from income statement

Income		Expenses	
Debits = reductions	Credits = increases	Debits = increases	Credits = reductions
	Interest payments received on member loans, investment income, fees, service charges	Payment of salaries, taxes, rent, bills, dividend expense, league dues	

Before we go on to the next step in the accounting process, you might want to prove to yourself that recording equal amounts of debits and credits will indeed maintain the balance sheet equation. Complete activity 2.1.

Figure 2.4 shows the debit/credit convention along with the basic equations of the balance sheet and income statement. Keep in mind that the net income is transferred to the equity account undivided earnings. Make up any combination of debits and credits in the five types of accounts. After you plug in the amounts, calculate any net income and transfer it to equity. Then calculate the balance sheet equation. You can get any dollar value for the equation, but as long as the amounts of debits

Basic Accounting

RECORDING TRANSACTIONS

Activity 2.1 Maintaining the Balance Sheet Equation

Determine the net balance in the cash account shown in transaction 5 in this chapter. Then add all the credits and all the debits in each of the T accounts shown in transactions 1 to 5 to prove the balance sheet equation.

Total debits = _____

Total credits = _____

Answers appear in appendix A.

and credits match (and you add correctly), the two halves of the balance sheet equation will match.

Posting to a Ledger

After transactions are analyzed and recorded in a journal, they are transferred, or posted, to a ledger. Because posting is the last time each individual transaction is recorded, ledgers are sometimes called books of final entry.

Just as different businesses may use different types of journals, they may also use a variety of ledgers. The most basic ledger is the **general ledger,** which is a collection of all the accounts of a business. Here we'll discuss only the general ledger. Other types of ledgers are covered in chapter 7.

The general ledger contains the same information as the general journal, but it's organized by account rather than by transaction to make preparation of the financial statements easier.

In a manual accounting system, the general ledger is usually a loose-leaf book with a separate page for each account. Depending on the complexity of the business, it may have a dozen or several hundred individual accounts. The sequence of the accounts in the general ledger matches the sequence of accounts on the financial statements, with income statement accounts listed before balance sheet accounts. The account name and number appear at the top of each ledger page. There are columns for the date, an explanation of the transaction, a posting reference, debits, credits, and the balance (figure 2.5). Remember that each entry on a page of a general ledger shows only one element of a financial transaction. The other portions of the exchange are shown in other accounts, and only the journal shows which combination of ledger entries represents a single transaction.

Notice that the explanation column in figure 2.5 is blank. This column may be used to explain an unusual transaction, but it is generally left blank since the details are already noted in the journal.

The posting reference column (P/R) in both the journal and ledger are filled in when a transaction is posted. In the ledger, the P/R column should show the page number in the journal where the transaction is originally recorded. The J1 noted in figure 2.5 refers to page 1 of the journal shown in figure 2.3. In the journal, the P/R column is filled in with the number of the account to which each element of the transaction is posted. The references make it easy to match entries in the two record books. This P/R procedure also helps prevent the error of posting the same transaction more than once. If you compare figures 2.3 and 2.5, you can see the last three transactions in figure 2.3 haven't been posted yet. That's why only the first two transactions in figure 2.3 have entries in the P/R column.

Figure 2.3 Journal Entries for Royal Credit Union

Page 1

Date	Account Titles and Explanation	P/R	Debit	Credit
20XX				
Oct. 1	Cash	730	10,000	
	Member shares	900		10,000
	Opening share deposits			
Oct. 5	Investments	740	9,000	
	Cash	730		9,000
	Purchase U.S. government obligations			
Nov. 16	Furniture and equipment		4,000	
	Notes payable			3,500
	Cash			500
	Purchase personal computer and laser printer from SuperComputers Inc.			
Dec. 1	Cash		900	
	Interest income			900
	Interest received on investments			
Dec. 1	Rent		100	
	Cash			100
	December rent to Royal Manufacturing			

Basic Accounting

RECORDING TRANSACTIONS

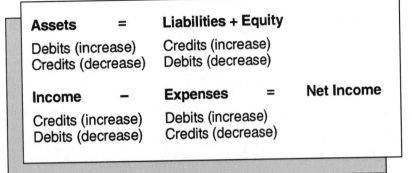

Figure 2.4 Debits/Credits and Financial Statement Equations

Figure 2.6 shows the corresponding elements of a single journal entry and its two general ledger entries.

The Normal Balance

The balance column in the general ledger does not indicate whether the balance is a debit or a credit. To perform the next step in the accounting process—the trial balance—you need to be familiar with the normal balance of each type of account. Normally, the balance in an account matches the way the account is increased—a debit for assets or expenses; a credit for liabilities, equity, or income (figure 2.7). To indicate that an account balance is opposite its normal balance, the total is shown in brackets, such as ($562).

Note: The normal balance also determines which column should show the balance in a T account. For example, cash is an asset account; its normal balance is a debit. Thus, the balance in the T account for cash should be shown in the debit (left) column.

```
            Cash
   10,000  |  9,000
      900  |    500
           |    100
   ─────────
    1,300
```

Test your knowledge of posting journal entries to a general ledger by completing activity 2.2.

Figure 2.5 General Ledger

Date	Explanation	P/R	Debit	Credit	Balance
Cash					Account No. 730
20XX					
Oct. 1		J1	10,000		10,000
Oct. 5		J1		9,000	1,000

Activity 2.2 Posting to a Ledger

The general journal for a small business, J.C. Carpentry, owned by sole proprietor, Jerrold Corcoran, has the following entries:

Page 1

Date	Account/Explanation	P/R	Debit	Credit
07/01/XX	Rent		1,000	
	Cash			1,000
	July rent to Simon Associates			
07/03/XX	Salaries		2,400	
	Cash			2,400
	Biweekly wages to Peter Matthews, Mark Lucas			
07/07/XX	Cash		3,215	
	Accounts receivable			3,215
	Payment received on account from Mary Walker			
07/09/XX	Utilities		457	
	Cash			457
	Paid to Pilot Gas & Electric for June			
07/10/XX	Equipment		3,000	
	Notes payable			2,500
	Cash			500
	Purchase saw from Carpentry Specialties			
07/15/XX	Accounts receivable		2,750	
	Carpentry services			2,750
	Invoiced Judy James for kitchen cabinets			
07/15/XX	Supplies		100	
	Cash			100
	Purchase hinges from Lumber Towne			

Post these journal entries to the appropriate general ledger accounts for J.C. Carpentry.

(continued)

Activity 2.2 Posting to a Ledger (continued)

General Ledger for J.C. Carpentry

Carpentry Services — Account No. 110

Date	Explanation	P/R	Debit	Credit	Balance

Salaries — Account No. 210

Date	Explanation	P/R	Debit	Credit	Balance

Rent — Account No. 220

Date	Explanation	P/R	Debit	Credit	Balance

Utilities — Account No. 230

Date	Explanation	P/R	Debit	Credit	Balance

Supplies — Account No. 240

Date	Explanation	P/R	Debit	Credit	Balance

(continued)

Activity 2.2 Posting to a Ledger (continued)

Date	Explanation	Cash P/R	Debit	Credit	Account No. 310 Balance

Date	Explanation	Accounts Receivable P/R	Debit	Credit	Account No. 320 Balance

Date	Explanation	Equipment P/R	Debit	Credit	Account No. 330 Balance

Date	Explanation	Notes Payable P/R	Debit	Credit	Account No. 410 Balance

Answers appear in appendix A.

Basic Accounting
RECORDING TRANSACTIONS

Figure 2.6 Posting to the General Ledger

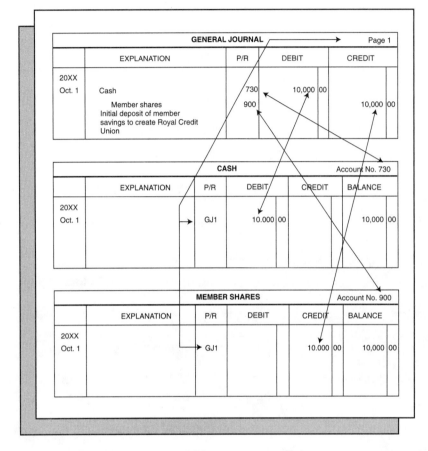

Figure 2.7 The Normal Balance of Each Type of Account

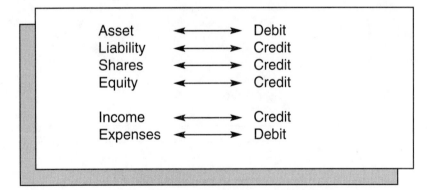

The Trial Balance

A trial balance is one means to check the accuracy of posting entries. It's a listing of all accounts in the order they appear in the general ledger, with their balances recorded as debits or credits according to the normal balance of the account. Since each transaction is recorded as equal amounts of debits and credits, the balances from general ledger accounts should also add up to equal amounts of debits and credits. That's what you look for in a trial balance. The sum of the debit balances should equal the sum of the credit balances. If the totals don't match, a mistake has been made. Figure 2.8 shows what Royal Credit Union's trial balance would look like after all the transactions from figure 2.3 are posted.

A trial balance doesn't prove the absolute accuracy of accounting entries, only that an equal amount of debits and credits were recorded. It would not, for example, identify an amount posted to the wrong account.

Despite its limitations, however, the trial balance is an important tool for maintaining the accuracy of an organization's financial records. If an error is indicated, you must find and correct the problem before proceeding to the next step in the accounting process.

A trial balance can be prepared at any time. However, it's routinely done as soon as all transactions for an accounting period have been recorded from the source documents to the journal and ledger. A trial balance prepared at this point is called an unadjusted trial balance. As you work your way through the next several chapters, you'll find two other points at which a trial balance is used to check the accuracy of accounting entries.

Prepare a trial balance by completing activity 2.3. In the next chapter, we'll prepare a trial balance worksheet.

Figure 2.8 Trial Balance

Royal Credit Union
Trial Balance
December 31, 20XX

	Debit	Credit
Interest income		$ 900
Rent	$ 100	
Cash	1,300	
Investments	9,000	
Furniture and equipment	4,000	
Notes payable		3,500
Shares		10,000
Total	$14,400	$14,400

Basic Accounting
RECORDING TRANSACTIONS

Activity 2.3 Preparing a Trial Balance

Turn to activity 2.2 and prepare a trial balance based on the balances in each of the general ledger accounts for J.C. Carpentry.

J.C. Carpentry
Trial Balance
July 15, 20XX

	Debit	Credit
Carpentry services		
Salaries		
Rent		
Utilities		
Supplies		
Cash		
Accounts receivable		
Equipment		
Notes payable		
Total		

Answers appear in appendix A.

Chapter 3 Recording Adjustments and Preparing the Trial Balance Worksheet

We introduced the first steps in the accounting cycle in the last chapter. Transactions from source documents are journalized and then posted to the general ledger. Given the need for timely information from the accounting system and the number of transactions most businesses have, the recording of transactions usually takes place throughout an accounting period. A trial balance can be used at any time to check the accuracy of the entries. However, a trial balance is also the first procedure performed at the end of the accounting period, as you get ready to prepare the financial statements and close the books.

In this chapter, we move on to the step after the trial balance—making adjustments.

The Accrual Basis of Accounting

To understand why adjustments are needed, you need to understand another basic accounting issue. We said earlier that an accountant must decide *when* to recognize transactions. Under generally accepted accounting principles, a business has two basic options. It can choose to recognize income and expenses only when cash changes hands, or it can recognize income and expenses in the accounting

Objectives

> **Upon completion of this chapter, you will be able to**
> 1. explain the difference between cash and accrual accounting;
> 2. prepare adjusting entries for accrued investment income, prepaid expenses, depreciation, and accrued expenses;
> 3. prepare a trial balance worksheet.

period when they are earned or incurred, regardless of when cash changes hands. The first option is the **cash basis** of accounting. The second option is the **accrual basis** of accounting.

Employee compensation provides a good illustration. Most businesses have a week or two lag time between the time employees actually work and the day they get paid for that work. If the payday is in the same accounting period as the time worked, the payroll expense is simply recorded on the day the checks are written under either method of accounting. But if the work is done during one accounting period and checks aren't written until the next period, the cash and accrual methods treat the payroll expense differently. Under the cash method, the payroll is considered an expense for the later accounting period. Under the accrual method, the payroll is considered an expense for the

Basic Accounting

RECORDING ADJUSTMENTS AND PREPARING THE TRIAL BALANCE WORKSHEET

first period because that's when the obligation to pay was incurred. To record this obligation on the books for the first period, the business has to make a special entry in the journal and ledger. This type of entry is known as an adjusting entry, or simply an adjustment.

The cash method of accounting is obviously easier, but the accrual method produces financial statements that more accurately reflect the true position of the business. The cash method is used primarily by small businesses. Most credit unions use the accrual method.

Adjusting Entries

Adjustments change a business's books from a cash basis to an accrual basis. Entries are made at the end of an accounting period, after all the usual transactions are recorded and before the financial statements are prepared. Some types of adjustments, such as depreciation and employee compensation, are common to most businesses on the accrual method. Others, such as a credit union's dividends payable, may be unique to a particular type of business. Since the types of transactions a business has don't change often, the types of adjusting entries used from period to period don't change much either.

Each adjusting entry is designed to revise an income or expense account. One portion of the double entry for each adjustment is recorded in the appropriate income or expense account, often the same account used for day-to-day transactions. The other portion of the double entry is recorded in a special balance sheet account that is used only for the adjustments.

To illustrate the adjusting process, we'll start with the trial balance of Lakeview Credit Union, shown in figure 3.1, and explain the major adjusting entries that would typically be made by a credit union at the end of an accounting period. They fall into four general categories: accrued investment income, prepaid expenses, depreciation, and accrued expenses.

Summarize your understanding of the accrual method of accounting in activity 3.1.

Figure 3.1 Unadjusted Trial Balance

Lakeview Credit Union
12/31/XX
Unadjusted Trial Balance

	Dr.	Cr.
Interest on loans		$20,620
Fees and charges		833
Salaries expense	$7,500	
Utilities expense	350	
Data processing expense	550	
Stationery and supplies expense	500	
Loans to members	1,850,000	
Cash	245,620	
Investments	100,000	
Prepaid rent	1,800	
Prepaid insurance	4,000	
Furniture and equipment	20,000	
Accounts payable		10,000
Regular shares		1,544,000
Share draft accounts		400,000
Regular reserves		135,000
Undivided earnings		119,867
	2,230,320	2,230,320

34

Basic Accounting

RECORDING ADJUSTMENTS AND PREPARING THE TRIAL BALANCE WORKSHEET

Activity 3.1 Understanding Accrual Accounting

1. What is the difference between the cash method and the accrual method of accounting?

2. What is the advantage of each method?

3. What method is used at your credit union?

Accrued Income on Investments

The first account we will analyze is income on investments.

Assume the Lakeview Credit Union has $100,000 invested in U.S. government obligations earning 8 percent interest. Investment income has been received through November 30, but no income has been received during December. Accrual accounting requires that the investment income earned during each accounting period be recorded as income, even though a cash payment has not been received. Assume also that Lakeview, like most credit unions, prepares financial statements monthly. What adjusting entry would need to be made for investment income at the end of December?

The calculation for investment income earned during December would be:

$$\text{Interest} = \text{Principal} \times \text{Rate} \times \text{Time}$$
$$I = (\$100,000)(.08)(.083)$$
$$I = \$664$$

Basic Accounting
RECORDING ADJUSTMENTS AND PREPARING THE TRIAL BALANCE WORKSHEET

In this equation, the rate of 8 percent (.08) is an annual rate, so the time—the month of December—is expressed as one month out of twelve: $1/12 = .083$.

The element of this transaction that will appear on the income statement is an increase (credit) in investment income. The matching balance sheet entry will go into an asset account set up specifically for this type of adjustment, called accrued investment income. The journal entry will look like this:

	Debit	Credit
Accrued investment income	664	
Investment income		664

Since neither the investment income account nor the accrued investment account appeared on the trial balance in figure 3.1, you know they had balances of zero. After the adjustment is posted, the balances will both be $664.

```
    Accrued
Investment Income        Investment Income
    664        |                     |    664
```

Prepaid Expenses

Prepaid expenses refer to payments made prior to receiving goods or services. At the end of an accounting period, these accounts must be analyzed and adjusted for the goods or services that have been received to-date. There are two prepaid items on Lakeview Credit Union's trial balance that we will analyze—prepaid rent and prepaid insurance.

Prepaid Rent

Lakeview Credit Union rents office space for $900 per month. Assume that on November 21, 20XX, Lakeview Credit Union made a rent payment of $1,800 for the months of December and January. When the payment was made, cash was credited and prepaid rent was debited for $1,800. An adjusting entry is needed at the end of December to record December's rent expense. The proper adjusting entry is to debit rent expense and credit prepaid rent for the $900.

	Debit	Credit
Rent expense	900	
Prepaid rent		900

Note that rent expense did not appear in the trial balance in figure 3.1 as no rent payment was made in December.

This adjusting entry recognizes the rent expense for the month and decreases the balance in the rent asset account. The general ledger accounts affected by the adjusting entry would appear as shown here.

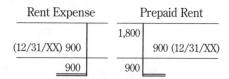

Prepaid Insurance

This account represents the value of the unexpired portion of insurance premiums that will be charged to expense at a subsequent date. Lakeview Credit Union made an insurance payment of $12,000 for the year beginning April 1, 20XX, and ending March 31 of the following year. This payment was charged to prepaid insurance and needs to be adjusted at the end of each month. At the end of each month, 1/12 of the payment must be expensed. The adjusting entry to record

Basic Accounting

RECORDING ADJUSTMENTS AND PREPARING THE TRIAL BALANCE WORKSHEET

December's expense would be made on December 31, as shown here.

	Debit	Credit
Insurance expense	1,000	
Prepaid insurance		1,000

The general ledger accounts would appear as follows after the adjustment has been posted:

Insurance Expense	Prepaid Insurance
	4,000
1,000	1,000
1,000	3,000

Note: The prepaid insurance balance was $12,000 on April 1, just after the premium payment was made. The adjustments in the eight months between April 1 and December 1 reduced prepaid insurance by $8,000 to the balance of $4,000 shown in figure 3.1. After the December adjustment, $3,000 remains in the prepaid account to be expensed in the next three months.

Depreciation

When a credit union purchases an expensive fixed asset, such as a computer or a building, it must allocate the cost of the fixed asset over the period of time the asset will be used. By allocating the cost of fixed assets over their useful life, the credit union can more accurately match its revenues with the costs associated with earning that revenue. Two accounts are used to distribute the cost of a fixed asset—depreciation expense from the income statement, and accumulated depreciation from the balance sheet. To understand how this distribution takes place, we will analyze the furniture and equipment account of Lakeview Credit Union. For now, we'll keep the example simple. Chapter 5 covers depreciation in greater detail.

Assume Lakeview Credit Union rents a furnished office and prior to December did not have any fixed assets of its own. On December 1, Lakeview purchased furniture and equipment for a total cost of $20,000. The entry that was made at the time of purchase was:

	Debit	Credit
Furniture and equipment	20,000	
Cash		20,000

This transaction is already reflected in the trial balance in figure 3.1. We will assume the furniture and equipment has a useful life of ten years and is to be depreciated evenly over its life. The amount of depreciation expense for each month is calculated by dividing $20,000 by 120 months (10 years) to get $167/month. The journal entry to record the depreciation expense for the month covered in figure 3.1 is:

	Debit	Credit
Depreciation expense	167	
Accumulated depreciation		167

Depreciation expense reflects the part of the cost of a fixed asset that is assigned to the current period. The accumulated depreciation account is used to

> Two accounts are used to distribute the cost of a fixed asset—depreciation expense from the income statement, and accumulated depreciation from the balance sheet.

Basic Accounting
RECORDING ADJUSTMENTS AND PREPARING THE TRIAL BALANCE WORKSHEET

keep track of how much of the total cost has been expensed since the item(s) were purchased. Accumulated depreciation is known as a contra account because its balance is subtracted from the fixed-asset account with which it is associated. Accumulated depreciation is listed with assets on the balance sheet, but its normal balance is a credit, rather than a debit. Lakeview's general ledger accounts would reflect the following balances at the end of December:

Furniture and Equipment	Accumulated Depreciation Furniture and Equipment	Depreciation Expense
20,000	167 (12/31)	167
20,000	167	167

The balance sheet at the end of the year will show the asset of furniture and equipment less its accumulated depreciation, while the income statement will reflect the depreciation expense.

Accrued Expenses

To allocate expenses to the proper accounting period, other accrued expense accounts must be established. The amounts to be established in these accounts usually are not yet due but are recorded to assign expenses to the periods to which they apply. Two such accounts are salaries payable and accrued dividends payable.

Salaries Payable

Salaries that are earned but not yet paid are recorded in salaries payable account at the end of the period. Salaries payable is a liability account. Lakeview Credit Union pays its employees every two weeks. Assume the employees have been paid through December 24 but will not receive another check until January 7. The amount of wages earned during December must be expensed in December. Under the assumption that the wages earned between December 24 and the end of the year amount to $3,000, the adjusting entry would be:

	Debit	Credit
Salaries expense	3,000	
Salaries payable		3,000

In all of the previous examples, the account balances were zero before the adjustments were made. In this case, the credit union had already recorded $7,500 in salaries expense for December. After posting the indicated adjustment, the general ledger would reflect the total salary expense of $10,500 in addition to the $3,000 liability for salaries payable.

Salaries Expense	Salaries Payable
7,500	
(12/31) 3,000	3,000 (12/31)
10,500	3,000

Accrued Dividends Payable

Accrued dividends payable is used to reflect the amount of dividends that are due and payable

Basic Accounting
RECORDING ADJUSTMENTS AND PREPARING THE TRIAL BALANCE WORKSHEET

to the members. Assume that on December 31, 20XX, Lakeview Credit Union has dividends due to its members in the amount of $8,000 for the month of December. This dividend will be paid on January 2, but it is actually an expense that relates to December. Therefore, on December 31, 20XX, the following adjusting entry must be made:

	Debit	Credit
Dividends expense	8,000	
Dividends payable		8,000

Since both accounts had a balance of zero before the adjustment, the ledger entries would show only the $8,000.

Dividends Expense	Dividends Payable
	8,000
(12/31) 8,000	
8,000	8,000

What adjusting entries are made at your credit union? Complete activity 3.2.

The Adjusted Trial Balance

Once all of the adjustments are recorded in the journal and posted to the ledger, an adjusted trial balance can be prepared. The adjusted trial balance will show the correct year-end balance for each account. Lakeview Credit Union's adjusted trial balance is shown in figure 3.2.

As a result of the adjustments, figure 3.2 shows nine accounts that weren't listed in figure 3.1. You may wonder how the sequence of these new accounts was determined.

> The adjusted trial balance will show the correct year-end balance for each account.

In all likelihood, the new accounts probably aren't new at all. Lakeview has probably used all of them in previous accounting periods, so the accounts were already set up in the general ledger. In any trial balance, the accounts match their general ledger sequence. The general ledger, in turn, is set up to match the sequence of accounts on financial statements, with income statement accounts listed first.

In the great majority of accounting systems, accounts are grouped for ease of use so that income accounts are one group, expenses another group, assets a third group, and so on. Within any group of accounts in the ledgers, the order of accounts is determined by the credit union.

When producing official reports for external users, generally accepted accounting principles provide guidance regarding which assets are reported before others. For reports to be used internally, most accountants list first those accounts they consider most important to the financial performance of the business.

Preparing a Worksheet

Many details are involved in a credit union's end-of-period adjusting process; it is easy to make errors. One way to minimize errors and simplify

Basic Accounting

RECORDING ADJUSTMENTS AND PREPARING THE TRIAL BALANCE WORKSHEET

Activity 3.2 Adjusting Entries

> Talk with the person at your credit union who is responsible for preparing the financial statements and find out what adjusting entries are made. List your findings.
>
> _____
> _____
> _____
> _____
> _____
> _____
> _____
> _____
> _____

procedures is to list all adjusting entries on a trial balance worksheet and check them for accuracy and completeness before recording the entries on the books. A worksheet also allows you to see the effects of proposed adjustments on the financial statements before the entries are recorded. The completed worksheet is later used to prepare the financial statements and closing entries of the credit union. (These are discussed in the next chapter.)

The worksheet is a working paper used by an accountant at the end of an accounting period. Figure 3.3 shows a worksheet prepared for Lakeview Credit Union. It contains a column to list the accounts from the general ledger and has five pairs of money columns. The money columns are in pairs so that debits and credits can be separated. The first pair of money columns is used to record the unadjusted trial balance of the credit union. The amounts are taken directly from the general ledger. Note, though, the list of account names includes all accounts where adjustments can be expected, even if they have a balance of zero at first. As you review the unadjusted trial balance, decide which accounts need to be adjusted. The adjustments are noted in the second pair of money columns. Each adjustment is referenced by a letter, so that related debits and credits can be identified. The debit and credit columns for the adjustments are totaled to ensure that debits and credits are equal.

RECORDING ADJUSTMENTS AND PREPARING THE TRIAL BALANCE WORKSHEET

Once the adjustments are recorded on the worksheet, they are combined with the trial balance amounts. The new adjusted balance is recorded in the third pair of money columns on the worksheet. The total debits and credits for the adjusted trial balance should match. If they don't, you have an error in one of the first two pairs of columns. When the adjusted trial balance is correct, the account balances are separated into the income statement accounts (the fourth column pair) and the balance sheet accounts (the fifth column pair).

The income statement columns reflect the actual revenues and expenses of the current accounting period. The debits represent the expenses of the period, while the credits represent the income of the period. The difference between the total debits and credits in the income statement columns is the net income or loss of the period. If the total credits are greater than the debits, the business has a net income. On the other hand, if total debits are greater than total credits, the business has a net loss. Lakeview shows a net income of $150.

The last two money columns on the worksheet are the balance sheet columns. The balance sheet columns represent the adjusted balances in the assets, liabilities, member shares, and equity accounts. When the two balance sheet columns are totaled on the worksheet, the debits and credits will not be equal. The difference between the debits and credits in the balance sheet columns should equal the net income or loss from the income statement columns. The equality of these two amounts is an indication that the amounts listed in the adjusted trial balance columns have been properly

Figure 3.2 Adjusted Trial Balance

Lakeview Credit Union
12/31/XX
Adjusted Trial Balance

	Dr.	Cr.
Interest on loans		$20,620
Investment income		664
Fees and charges		833
Salaries expense	$10,500	
Rent expense	900	
Utilities expense	350	
Data processing expense	550	
Stationery and supplies expense	500	
Insurance expense	1,000	
Depreciation expense	167	
Dividends expense	8,000	
Loans to members	1,850,000	
Cash	245,620	
Investments	100,000	
Prepaid rent	900	
Prepaid insurance	3,000	
Furniture and equipment	20,000	
Accumulated depreciation, furniture, and equipment		167
Accrued investment income	664	
Accounts payable		10,000
Dividends payable		8,000
Salaries payable		3,000
Regular shares		1,544,000
Share draft accounts		400,000
Regular reserves		135,000
Undivided earnings		119,867
	$2,242,151	$2,242,151

Basic Accounting
RECORDING ADJUSTMENTS AND PREPARING THE TRIAL BALANCE WORKSHEET

carried over to the income statement and balance sheet columns.

When all adjusting entries are listed correctly and the totals in the financial statement columns mesh as they should, you are ready to prepare the financial statements. Note that so far the adjusting entries appear only on the worksheet. They have not yet been entered into the journal or ledger. This is done after the financial statements are prepared.

Summarize your understanding of the trial balance worksheet by completing activity 3.3.

In this chapter we've introduced the accrual method of accounting, which provides the most accurate picture of the financial condition of a business. The accrual basis of accounting requires that accounts be analyzed for adjustments before the financial statements are prepared. A trial balance worksheet can make the adjustment process easier and helps to ensure accuracy. Once the worksheet is complete, the general ledger can be updated by journalizing and posting the adjusting entries. This is the subject of the next chapter.

When all adjusting entries are listed correctly and the totals in the financial statement columns mesh as they should, you are ready to prepare the financial statements.

Activity 3.3 Understanding the Trial Balance Worksheet

1. What is the purpose of the trial balance worksheet?

2. When are the financial statements prepared?

Basic Accounting

RECORDING ADJUSTMENTS AND PREPARING THE TRIAL BALANCE WORKSHEET

Figure 3.3 Trial Balance Worksheet

Account	Unadjusted Trial Balance Dr.	Unadjusted Trial Balance Cr.	Adjustments Dr.		Adjustments Cr.		Adjusted Trial Balance Dr.	Adjusted Trial Balance Cr.	Income Statement Dr.	Income Statement Cr.	Balance Sheet Dr.	Balance Sheet Cr.
Interest on loans		20620						20620		20620		
Investment income		- 0 -			(a)	664		664		664		
Fees & charges		833						833		833		
Salaries expense	7500		(e)	3000			10500		10500			
Rent expense	- 0 -		(b)	900			900		900			
Utilities expense	350						350		350			
Data processing expense	550						550		550			
Stationery/supplies	500						500		500			
Insurance expense	- 0 -		(c)	1000			1000		1000			
Depreciation expense	- 0 -		(d)	167			167		167			
Dividends expense	- 0 -		(f)	8000			8000		8000			
Loans to members	1850000						1850000				1850000	
Cash	245620						245620				245620	
Investments	100000						100000				100000	
Prepaid rent	1800				(b)	900	900				900	
Prepaid insurance	4000				(c)	1000	3000				3000	
Furniture & equipment	20000						20000				20000	
Acc. deprec. furn. & equip.		- 0 -			(d)	167		167				167
Acc. invest. income	- 0 -		(a)	664			664				664	
Accounts payable		10000						10000				10000
Dividends payable		- 0 -			(f)	8000		8000				8000
Salaries payable		- 0 -			(e)	3000		3000				3000
Regular shares		1544000						1544000				1544000
Share draft accounts		400000						400000				400000
Regular reserves		135000						135000				135000
Undivided earnings		119867						119867				119867
Totals	2230320	2230320		13731		13731	2242151	2242151	21967	22117	2220184	2220034
Net income									150			150
									22117	22117	2220184	2220184

(a) To accrue interest receivable on investments
(b) To adjust prepaid rent for December expense
(c) To adjust prepaid insurance for the December expense
(d) To record depreciation expense for December
(e) To accrue salary expense for the last week of December
(f) To record dividend payable at 12-31-XX

43

Chapter 4 Financial Statements and the Closing of Accounts

We illustrated the preparation of adjusting entries for a credit union in chapter 3. Adjusting entries are necessary at the end of the accounting period to properly reflect income and expenses. Once all of the adjusting entries have been noted, the financial statements can be prepared from an adjusted trial balance.

Preparing Financial Statements from a Worksheet

An accountant is able to prepare the income statement and balance sheet directly from the corresponding columns of the trial balance worksheet. As we've said, preparing financial statements at this point allows an accountant to analyze the financial statements before finalizing the adjusting entries in the general ledger. The income statement and balance sheet shown in figures 4.1 and 4.2 were prepared directly from the worksheet in figure 3.3.

These financial statements include much more detail than the very simple examples presented in chapter 1, yet they follow the same basic formats.

The income statement is prepared first since the net income or loss from the income statement is required to complete the balance sheet.

Objectives

Upon completion of this chapter, you will be able to

1. prepare an income statement and balance sheet for a credit union;
2. prepare the closing entries for a credit union;
3. describe the content and purpose of a post-closing trial balance;
4. state the required steps in the accounting cycle.

Figure 4.1 Income Statement

Lakeview Credit Union
Income Statement
For the Month Ended December 31, 20XX

Income:		
Interest on loans	$20,620	
Investment income	664	
Fees and charges	833	
Total income		$22,117
Expenses:		
Salaries expense	$10,500	
Rent expense	900	
Utilities expense	350	
Data processing expense	550	
Stationery and supplies expense	500	
Insurance expense	1,000	
Depreciation expense	167	
Dividends expense	8,000	
Total expenses		21,967
Net Income		$150

FINANCIAL STATEMENTS AND THE CLOSING OF ACCOUNTS

Figure 4.2 Balance Sheet

Lakeview Credit Union
Balance Sheet
December 31, 20XX

Assets:		
Loans to members		$1,850,000
Cash		245,620
Investments		100,000
Prepaid rent		900
Prepaid insurance		3,000
Furniture and equipment	$20,000	
Less accumulated depreciation	167	19,833
Accrued investment income		664
Total Assets		**$2,220,017**
Liabilities:		
Accounts payable	$10,000	
Dividends payable	$8,000	
Salaries payable	3,000	
Total Liabilities		**$21,000**
Member Shares:		
Regular shares	$1,544,000	
Share draft accounts	400,000	
Total Member Shares		**$1,944,000**
Equity:		
Regular reserves	$135,000	
Undivided earnings	120,017	
Total Equity		**$255,017**
Total Liabilities, Member Shares, and Equity		**$2,220,017**

The Income Statement

As you recall, the income statement shows all the income earned during an accounting period, less the expenses incurred in generating that income. The income statement's title should always indicate the length of time the statement represents. Account balances are taken from the adjusted trial balance. Lakeview has a net income of $150.

Figure 4.3 presents the same income statement prepared on a standard federal credit union form. Note that the account types on the form are different from those used so far in this course. For example, the $1,250 amount for "office occupancy expenses" in figure 4.3 is made up of $350 utilities expense plus $900 rent expense in figure 4.1. Accountants must frequently submit financial information to different internal users or external parties, with each different user desiring a different format for the information. In general, accounting systems are designed to record a great deal of detail to satisfy the various requests for information. The accountant must then combine the detailed accounts in ways that meet the needs of each user.

Note also that the income statement presented in figure 4.3 shows only the month-end information. To be complete, the statement should also include financial information for the current year and current period (such as quarter), as well as other information requested.

The Balance Sheet

The balance sheet in figure 4.2 places liabilities, shares, and equity below assets, rather than beside them as shown previously. Either format is acceptable. The amounts for the balance sheet accounts in figure 4.2 are taken from the adjusted trial balance shown on the worksheet.

Basic Accounting
FINANCIAL STATEMENTS AND THE CLOSING OF ACCOUNTS

Figure 4.3 Income Statement

STATEMENT OF INCOME FOR PERIOD ENDED December 31, 20XX

Lakeview _____ CREDIT UNION

Internal Use Only — Acct. Code No. _____ Charter # _____ or Ins. Cert. # _____
Report Type _____

Ref. #	Item	Month Dec. Amount $ ¢	Period From ___ To Date. Amount $ ¢	Year To Date Amount $ ¢	Acct. Code No.
	INTEREST INCOME				
42.	Interest on Loans (Gross)	20,620			
43.	(Less) Interest Refunded				
44.	Income from Investments	664			
45.	Total Interest Income (Sum of 42-44 less 43)	21,284			
	INTEREST EXPENSE				
46.	Dividends	8,000			
47.	Interest on Borrowed Money				
48.	Total Interest Expense	8,000			
49.	Net Interest Income (Item 45 less 48)	13,284			
50.	Provision for Loan Losses				
51.	Provision for Unrealized Mutual Fund Losses				
52.	Net Interest Income after Provisions for Losses (Item 49 less 50 and 51)	13,284			
	OPERATING EXPENSES				
53.	Employee Compensation	10,500			
54.	Employee Benefits				
55.	Travel & Conference				
56.	Association Dues				
57.	Office Occupancy Expenses	1,250			
58.	Office Operation Expenses	1,667			
59.	Loan Servicing Expenses	550			
60.	Professional & Outside				
61.	Member Insurance				
62.	Operating Fees (Exam)				
63.	Misc. Operating Expense				
64.	Total Operating Expense (Sum of 65-66)	13,967			
	OTHER OPERATING INCOME				
65.	Operating Income	833			
66.	Trading Profits and Losses				
67.	Total Other Operating Income (Sum of 65-66)	833			
	NON-OPERATING INCOME				
68.	Gain (Loss) on Investments				
69.	Gain (Loss) on Disposition of Assets				
70.	Other Non-Operating Income (Expense)				
71.	Total Non-Operating Gains and Losses				
72.	Net Income (Sum of 52, 67, and 71 less 64)	150			

Refer to the Accompanying Statement of Reserves and Undivided Earnings for the Change in Undivided Earnings.

Ref. #	Item	CLASSIFICATION OF LOANS OUTSTANDING			Acct. Code No.
		A. Number	B. $ Amount ¢		
73.	Degree of Delinquency:				
	a. Current and less than 2 months				
	b. 2 to less than 6 months				
	c. 6 to less than 12 months				
	d. 12 months and over				
	e. Total loans (Sum of 73a thru 73d) (must equal 2)				
	MISCELLANEOUS INFORMATION				
74.	Number of members at end of month				
75.	Number of potential members				
	OTHER LOAN INFORMATION				
76.	Loans sold and being serviced by credit union				
77.	Real estate loans made during current year				
78.	Total loans made during current year (include real estate loans)				
79.	Total loans made since organization				
80.	Total loans charged off-since organization				
81.	Recovery of loans charged-off since organization				
82.	Net loans charged-off since organization				

We certify, to the best of our knowledge and belief, this statement and the related statements are true and correct and present fairly the financial position and the results of operations for the periods covered.

Certified corrected by: (PLEASE PRINT) _____ Telephone No. _____

Treasurer-Manager (Signature) _____ Date _____

President/Authorized Officer _____ Date _____

*Numbers in this column refer to notes to financial statements; Letters refer to supplementary schedules which are attached.

FCU 109B 11215 (Rev. 5/90) Updated 8/91

Basic Accounting

FINANCIAL STATEMENTS AND THE CLOSING OF ACCOUNTS

Figure 4.4 Balance Sheet (Statement of Financial Condition)

STATEMENT OF FINANCIAL CONDITION AS OF December 31, 20 XX — Lakeview CREDIT UNION

Internal Use Only / Report Type — Acct. Code No. 100 — Charter # or Ins. Cert. #

ASSETS

Ref.	Item	LOANS & CASH	$ Amount	Remaining Maturities A. 1 yr. or less	B. More than 1 yr.	¢	Acct. Code
	1.	Commercial and agricultural loans to members					
	a.	Real Estate loans to members (first lien), original maturity over 12 years					
	b.	Loan balance fully secured by shares					
	c.	All other loans to members (excluding a, b, c, above)	1,850,000				
	d.	Total loans to members (include items a, b, c, and d)	1,850,000				
	e.	All other loan accounts (excluding amts. in 1a, b, c, and d)					
	2.	Total loans (Sum of 1e and f)	1,850,000				
	3.	(Less) Allowance for loan losses					
	4.	Net loans outstanding (Sum of 2 less 3)	1,850,000				
	5.	Cash (cash on hand, petty cash, checking accts., etc.)	245,620				

Ref.	Item	INVESTMENTS (A + B = C)	Total C	Remaining Maturities A. 1 yr. or less	B. More than 1 yr.		
	6.	U.S. Gov. Obligations	100,000				
	7.	Federal Agency Securities					
	8.	Shares, Deposits & Certif. in Corp. Centrals					
	9.	Shares, deposits & certif. in other CUs, banks, S&Ls, & MSBs					
	10.	Other investments					
	11.	NCUSIF Capital Deposit					
	12.	Shares in Central Liquidity Facility (Direct or Indirect)					
	13.	(Less) Allowance for Investment securities					
	14.	Mutual funds, incl. common trust investments					
	15.	(Less) Allow. for common trust & mutual fund invstmt. losses					
	16.	Trading securities (at market)					
	17.	Net Investments (Sum of 6-12, 14 and 16, less 13 and 15)	100,000				

OTHER ASSETS

Ref.	Item		$				
	18.	Land and buildings (not of depreciation)					
	19.	Other fixed assets (net of depreciation)	19,833				
	20.	Monetary control reserve deposits					
	21.	All other assets	4,564				
	22.	TOTAL ASSETS (Sum of 4, 5, 17, and 18-21)	2,220,017				

FCU 109A 11214 (Rev. 10/90) (Updated 8/91)

LIABILITIES AND EQUITY

Ref.	Item	(A + B = C)	Remaining Maturities A. 1 yr. or less	B. More than 1 yr.	$ Amount C.	¢	Acct. Code
	23.	Notes Payable					
	24.	Reverse repurchase transactions			10,000		
	25.	Interest payable			8,000		
	26.	Accounts payable					
	27.	Dividends/Interest on shares/deposits payable					
	28.	Unapplied data processing exceptions			3,000		
	29.	All other liabilities					
	30.	TOTAL LIABILITIES (Sum of 23-29)			21,000		

Ref.	Item		Remaining Maturities A. 1 yr. or less	B. More than 1 yr.	$ Amount C.	¢	
	31. a.	Share certificates			400,000		
	b.	Share draft accounts					
	c.	Member's' deposits (SCU's only)					
	d.	IRA/Keogh & retirement accounts			1,544,000		
	e.	Other member savings					
	f.	Non-member savings					
	g.	Total savings/shares/deposits (Sum of 31a-31f)			1,944,000		
	32.	Regular/statutory reserves			135,000		
	33.	Investment valuation reserve (SCU's only)					
	34.	Special reserves					
	35.	Other reserves					
	36.	Undivided earnings			120,017		
	37.	Net Income (loss)					
	38.	TOTAL LIABILITIES AND EQUITY (Sum of 30, 31g and 32-27)			2,220,017		

Ref.	Item	MARKET VALUES OF INVESTMENTS	Remaining Maturities A. 1 yr. or less	B. More than 1 yr.	$ Amount C.	¢	
	39.	U.S. Government Obligations					
	40.	Federal Agency Securities					
	41.	All other investments					

* Numbers in this column refer to notes in financial statements, letters refer to supplementary schedules which are attached.

Printed in U.S.A. by Union Labor

However, the undivided earnings account on the balance sheet is a combination of the undivided earnings from the worksheet, plus the net income from the income statement, as shown:

Statement of Retained Earnings

Net income per income statement	$150
Undivided earnings per 12/31/XX trial balance	119,867
Undivided earnings per 12/31/XX balance sheet	$120,017

Figure 4.4 shows the balance sheet from figure 4.2 on the federal form. The federal form is titled Statement of Financial Condition, which is often used interchangeably with the title Balance Sheet. Again, as with the income statement, some accounts had to be combined to conform to the federal credit union format:

(a) Item 19 Other Fixed Assets (net of depreciation) includes:

Furniture and equipment	$20,000
Less accumulated deprec.	<167>
	$19,833

(b) Item 21 All Other Assets includes:

Prepaid rent	$900
Prepaid insurance	3,000
Accr. investment income	664
	$4,564

Journalizing Adjusting Entries

When the financial statements are prepared directly from the worksheet, the general ledger still reflects the balances as they appeared in the unadjusted trial balance column of the worksheet. To reflect the proper period-end balances in the general ledger, the adjusting entries now must be journalized in the appropriate journal and posted to the general ledger. Journal entries were presented in chapter 3. Once the adjusting entries are posted to the general ledger, the balances in the general ledger will be the same as they are in the adjusted trial balance column of the worksheet.

The posting of the adjusting entries to the general ledger is the final step in recording the transactions that took place during the accounting period. Before a new accounting period can be recorded, the accountant must close the books of the prior period.

Test your knowledge of how to prepare financial statements by completing activity 4.1.

Closing Entries

To close the books of an accounting period means to bring the balance of each income statement account to zero and to transfer the net income of the period to equity accounts in the general ledger.

The income statement accounts are referred to as the nominal or temporary accounts of a business. These nominal accounts have balances from transactions that take place only during a single accounting period, such as the month of

---

To close the books of an accounting period means to bring the balance of each income statement account to zero and to transfer the net income of the period to equity accounts in the general ledger.

Basic Accounting

FINANCIAL STATEMENTS AND THE CLOSING OF ACCOUNTS

Activity 4.1 Preparing Financial Statements

Read the following statements and mark each true (T) or false (F).

____ 1. Preparing the financial statements is the final step in the accounting cycle.

____ 2. The balance sheet is prepared first.

____ 3. The title of a balance sheet should indicate the accounting period covered by the balance sheet.

____ 4. Account balances that appear on the financial statements are taken from the adjusted trial balance.

____ 5. A statement of financial condition is also known as an income statement.

____ 6. Financial statements are prepared from the trial balance worksheet.

Answers appear in appendix A.

December in the Lakeview Credit Union example we've been using. At the end of each period, the nominal accounts are zeroed or closed out by transferring the net income for the period to the real accounts of the balance sheet. The balance sheet accounts are referred to as real accounts since they are more permanent—their balances are carried over from one accounting period to the next.

For most businesses, the actual recording of the closing entries is made in three steps and can be made directly from the income statement column of the worksheet. The first step is to close out the income accounts. This is accomplished by debiting each income account for an amount equal to its credit balance, and crediting a temporary income summary account. The second step is to close out the expense accounts by crediting each account for an amount equal to its balance and debiting the same temporary income summary account used to close out the income accounts.

The debits and credits offset each other, leaving a balance in the income summary account equal to the net income for the period. The third step is to transfer the net income from the income summary account to the undivided earnings account. When this transfer is completed, the balance in the general ledger for undivided earnings will match the amount already shown on the balance sheet for the end of the period.

Basic Accounting
FINANCIAL STATEMENTS AND THE CLOSING OF ACCOUNTS

This three-step process is sufficient for most businesses. However, the credit union Prompt Corrective Action regulation sometimes requires an additional entry. Under circumstances described in chapter 6, a credit union may be required to transfer an amount from its undivided earnings to the regular reserve account. This transfer would be the fourth step in the closing process.

Closing Entries Illustrated

To illustrate the four closing entries we've described we again refer to Lakeview Credit Union's trial balance worksheet (see figure 3.3). As previously mentioned, our closing entries will come from the income statement column of the worksheet.

Step 1: Closing the Income Accounts

The journal entry to close out the income accounts of Lakeview Credit Union for the month ended December 31, 20XX, would be:

		Debit	Credit
12/31/XX	Interest on loans	20,620	
	Investment income	664	
	Fees and charges	833	
	Income summary		22,117

Step 2: Closing the Expense Accounts

The journal entry to close out the expense accounts of Lakeview Credit Union for the month ended December 31, 20XX, would be:

		Debit	Credit
12/31/XX	Income summary	21,967	
	Salaries		10,500
	Rent		900
	Utilities		350
	Data processing		550
	Stationery and supplies		500
	Insurance		1,000
	Depreciation expense		167
	Dividends		8,000

These first two closing entries bring all of the income statement account balances to zero. When the journal entries are posted, the ledger account for income summary looks like this:

Income Summary	
To close out expenses 21,967	22,117 To close out income
	150

The income and expenses offset each other, leaving only the $150 net income. Both the normal balance and increases to the income summary account are recorded as credits.

Step 3: Closing the Income Summary Account

The journal entry to close out the income summary account for Lakeview Credit Union for the month ended December 31, 20XX, would be:

	Debit	Credit
Income summary	$150	
Undivided earnings		$150

Basic Accounting

FINANCIAL STATEMENTS AND THE CLOSING OF ACCOUNTS

This third entry brings the income summary account balance to zero and transfers the net income to the balance sheet account undivided earnings. The income summary account now appears as follows in the general ledger:

```
                Income Summary
                        | 22,117 To close out
                        |        income
To close out expenses   |
              21,967    |
To transfer net income  |
                 150    |
                        |
                        -0-
```

Step 4: Making a Reserve Transfer

Lakeview's fourth closing step is to record any regular reserve transfer it will make for December. Chapter 6 provides more information on regular reserves—when they are required and how to calculate the amount. For now, we'll assume Lakeview would like to add $1,100 to its regular reserve account. The journal entry would be:

		Debit	Credit
12/31/XX	Undivided earnings	1,100	
	Regular reserves		1,100

Both of these accounts are equity accounts, so the debit reduces undivided earnings and the credit increases regular reserves. After posting, the ledger accounts show the following balances:

```
Undivided Earnings      Regular Reserves
       | 120,017             | 135,000
 1,100 |                     |  1,100
       | 118,917             | 136,100
```

Since this regular reserve transfer is not reflected on the credit union's balance sheet see figure 4.2), the equity section of the statement should be revised to match the new account balances:

Equity:
Regular reserves	$136,100	
Undivided earnings	118,917	
Total equity		$255,017

The Accounts After Closing

Once all closing entries have been journalized and posted, the general ledger reflects the end-of-period balances of all the balance sheet accounts and contains a balance of zero in all of the income statement accounts. A trial balance prepared at the very end of the accounting cycle is called a postclosing trial balance. Figure 4.5 presents a postclosing trial balance for Lakeview Credit Union on December 31, 20XX.

Summarize your understanding of closing entries in activity 4.2.

The Accounting Cycle

Each period a credit union goes through a complete accounting cycle. Let's review the steps in that cycle in the order of occurrence.

1. *Journalizing.* The original recording of a transaction in a journal.
2. *Posting.* The process of copying the transaction from the journal to the general ledger.
3. *Preparing a trial balance.* The listing of all general ledger account balances to ensure equality of debits and credits.

Basic Accounting
FINANCIAL STATEMENTS AND THE CLOSING OF ACCOUNTS

4. *Preparing a worksheet.* Analyzing adjustments on a worksheet before recording them; distributing the adjusted account balances into the income statement and balance sheet columns of the worksheet.

5. *Preparing financial statements.* Taking the final account balances from the worksheet and preparing a formal income statement and balance sheet.

6. *Recording adjusting entries.* Journalizing the adjusting entries from the worksheet and posting the adjustments to the general ledger. The adjusting entries for a credit union includes transfers to regular reserves if any are made.

7. *Recording closing entries.* Journalizing the entries to zero out the account balances in all of the income statement accounts and transferring the net income to the balance sheet. Credit unions may also make an additional closing entry to transfer equity from undivided earnings to the regular reserve account.

8. *Preparing a postclosing trial balance.* The final step in the accounting cycle to ensure the accounts have been properly closed and the general ledger is ready for the next accounting period.

In this chapter we've revealed the final steps in the accounting cycle. The remaining chapters in this course provide more detail on specific areas of accounting.

Figure 4.5 Postclosing Trial Balance

Lakeview Credit Union
Postclosing Trial Balance
December 31, 20XX

Loans to members	$1,850,000	
Cash	245,620	
Investments	100,000	
Prepaid rent	900	
Prepaid insurance	3,000	
Furniture and equipment	20,000	
Acc. depreciation furn. and equip.		$167
Accrued investment income	664	
Accounts payable		10,000
Dividends payable		8,000
Salaries payable		3,000
Regular shares		1,544,000
Share draft accounts		400,000
Regular reserves		136,100
Undivided earnings		118,917
	$2,220,184	$2,220,184

Basic Accounting

FINANCIAL STATEMENTS AND THE CLOSING OF ACCOUNTS

Activity 4.2 Closing Entries

Answer the following questions about the process of closing a credit union's books.

1. Why are the books closed at the end of the accounting cycle?

2. Which accounts are a credit union's nominal accounts?

3. Which are the real accounts?

4. What is the income summary account?

5. How many steps are involved in closing the books at your credit union?

Chapter 5 Accounting for Fixed Assets

Fixed assets are property and equipment obtained by a credit union and used to provide services to members. The distinguishing feature of this type of property or equipment is that it is used in producing other assets or services over more than one year.

A good working example of this definition is the purchase of a building. A building has a useful life of more than one year. In addition, the building provides a means of efficiently producing other credit union assets and services, such as loans, the sale of traveler's checks, and the sale of insurance.

Because the item of property or equipment produces assets or services for more than one accounting period, it's necessary to allocate the cost of the fixed asset to the periods benefited. Periods benefited simply means the number of years we expect to use the item in the production of assets or services. As explained earlier, the process of allocating this cost to the periods benefited is called depreciation.

Depreciation is not a process of allocating physical deterioration or loss in value. Rather, it's a method of allocating the cost of an asset to the time period during which it helps to produce income.

Another way to visualize this process is to think of the asset's acquisition as the purchase of its usefulness. Depreciation then becomes a method of recognizing an expense as the estimated usefulness of the asset as consumed over time. For example, if we purchase a copier on January 1, 20XX, at a cost of $3,000 with an estimated service life of five years, we would use up one-fifth of the copier's usefulness on an annual basis. This amounts to $600 per year, or $50 per month. The appropriate dollar amount is recorded as depreciation expense in each accounting period.

Certain types of fixed assets can't be depreciated because their useful life can't be determined. Land, for example, can be used for an almost endless period. It is not depreciated.

Objectives

Upon completion of this chapter, you will be able to

1. **define fixed assets and depreciation;**
2. **determine the cost of fixed assets and compute depreciation using the straight-line method;**
3. **understand how fixed assets and depreciation affect a business's financial statements.**

Because the item of property or equipment produces assets or services for more than one accounting period, it's necessary to allocate the cost of the fixed asset to the periods benefited.

ACCOUNTING FOR FIXED ASSETS

The Cost of Fixed Assets

Fixed assets are recorded at cost. Generally, cost is simply the cash expenditure for an item. However, cost may also include a number of other expenditures to make the asset ready for its intended use. For example, the purchase of an in-house data processing system may include

- the invoice price;
- delivery and setup charges;
- sales tax (if applicable);
- special electrical connections, and so on.

The depreciable cost of a fixed asset is simply the total of all normal, reasonable, and necessary expenditures that make the item functional. Some expenditures should not be included in cost because they are not normal. For example, if a data processing system is dropped during installation and requires repairs, the repairs should be expensed.

The most common cost components of buildings and equipment are detailed here.

Description	Cost Components
Buildings	Purchase price/construction cost Architectural fees Legal fees Permits Construction period insurance Construction period interest
Furniture and equipment	Purchase price Delivery charges Sales tax (if applicable) Setup charges

Service Life

The service life of property and equipment is simply our best estimate of how long the asset will be used in a productive capacity. Estimated service lives for various asset categories have been established as part of generally accepted accounting principles and are stated in terms of acceptable ranges.

An accountant familiar with the conventions should establish the estimated service life used to depreciate an asset. The exact term used should be based on an understanding of the asset's productive capacity, potential for obsolescence, and ability to continue adequately meeting productive needs.

What assets does your credit union own, and what is their service life? Complete activity 5.1.

Calculating Depreciation

A number of depreciation methods can be used to allocate the cost of a fixed asset over its estimated service life. The approach most often used by credit unions is the straight-line method. However, before discussing depreciation methods, it's important to understand when the depreciation process should begin. Generally, you should begin depreciating a fixed asset as soon as you start using it for its intended function. The fact that the fixed asset may not be completely paid for is irrelevant.

Basic Accounting
ACCOUNTING FOR FIXED ASSETS

Activity 5.1 Investigating Fixed-Asset Service Life

Talk to your credit union's accountant for answers to the following questions.

What fixed assets are owned by your credit union? Check all that apply.

- ☐ Land
- ☐ Building
- ☐ Vehicle
- ☐ Furniture
- ☐ Equipment
- ☐ Leasehold improvements
- ☐ Other _____

What service life has been established for each of your credit union's fixed assets? List the asset and service life.

_____
_____
_____
_____
_____
_____

For example, if you construct a new building and actually open the doors for business on July 1, 20XX, depreciation begins at that date. Even though you may still have construction in process or owe amounts to the construction contractor, depreciation begins on the date on which an asset is substantially ready for its intended use.

Straight-Line Depreciation

In all of the depreciation examples we've presented so far, we've used the straight-line method to calculate the expense for each accounting period. This method of depreciation allocates the total asset cost, less estimated salvage value, equally over each accounting period in the asset's

57

Basic Accounting

ACCOUNTING FOR FIXED ASSETS

estimated service life. Salvage value represents an estimate of the value remaining at the end of an asset's service life. The straight-line depreciation method can be calculated using the following formula:

$$\frac{\text{(Asset cost} - \text{Estimated salvage value)}}{\text{Estimated service life}} = \text{Periodic depreciation expense}$$

To illustrate the use of this formula, assume we purchase a computer at a cost of $5,000, to which we assign an estimated service life of sixty months (five years). If we assume a salvage value of zero, the amount of depreciation to be recognized each month is calculated as follows:

$$\frac{(\$5,000.00 - \$0.00)}{60} = \$83.33$$

For purposes of our calculations, we assume that assets have an estimated salvage value of zero unless stated otherwise.

Calculate depreciation of fixed assets in activity 5.2.

Activity 5.2 Calculating Depreciation

Calculate the monthly depreciation for the following fixed assets.

Office Building:
    Cost = $200,000
    Salvage value = 0
    Service life = 30 years
    Depreciation expense = _____

Computer System:
    Cost = $75,000
    Salvage value = $5,000
    Service life = 5 years
    Depreciation expense = _____

Automobile:
    Cost = $14,500
    Salvage value = $4,000
    Service life = 3 years
    Depreciation expense = _____

Answers appear in appendix A.

Accounting for Fixed Asset Transactions

In an earlier chapter we explained the basic accounting entries required to record fixed assets and to make the period-end adjustment for depreciation. We'll review those accounting entries with a more complex example.

Assume that Big Sky Federal Credit Union makes the following fixed-asset purchases:

Date	Description	Cost
April 1, 20XX	Office building	$240,000
May 1, 20XX	Office furniture	60,000
June 1, 20XX	Equipment	21,000

The journal entries necessary to record the purchases of these items are at the top of the next column.

The credit union assigns the following lives to each of the fixed-asset purchases, in accordance with established guidelines:

	Service Life
Office building	480 months
Office furniture	120 months
Equipment	60 months

All of the fixed assets are depreciated using the straight-line method, assuming a salvage value of zero. The credit union's policy is to record depreciation quarterly.

		Debit	Credit
April 1, 20XX	Building	240,000	
	Cash		$48,000
	Mortgage payable		$192,000
May 1, 20XX	Furniture and equipment	60,000	
	Cash		$60,000
June 1, 20XX	Furniture and equipment	21,000	
	Cash		$21,000

Based on the purchase dates previously detailed, the initial amount of depreciation expense to be recorded on June 30 is calculated as follows:

Description	Cost	Service Life	Depreciation Expense per Month	No. of Months	Expense
Office building	$240,000	480	$500	3	$1,500
Office furniture	60,000	120	500	2	1,000
Equipment	21,000	60	350	1	350
					$2,850

The journal entry necessary to record the depreciation adjustment is:

	Debit	Credit
Depreciation Expense	2,850	
Accumulated depreciation—building		1,500
Accumulated depreciation—furniture and equipment		1,350

ACCOUNTING FOR FIXED ASSETS

Remember that the credit portion of the depreciation entry is recorded through a contra account, accumulated depreciation, rather than as a direct reduction of the asset account. After we review the way these accounts are shown on the balance sheet, we'll explain the advantage of the contra account.

Financial Statement Presentation of Fixed Assets

Fixed assets are presented on the credit union's statement of financial condition at cost less accumulated depreciation. The two components should be reflected as illustrated:

**Big Sky Federal Credit Union
(Partial) Statement
of Financial Condition
June 30, 20XX**

Cash		$500,000
Loans		9,950,000
Land		100,000
Building, furniture and equipment	$321,000	
Less: Accumulated depreciation	2,850	318,150

When balances are shown in this manner, the financial statement reader can get a much better understanding of the composition of the credit union's fixed assets. To most credit union directors or management officials, $25,000 of new fixed assets would convey something quite different from $100,000 of fixed assets with $75,000 of accumulated depreciation. If only the net value is shown in the credit union's statement of financial condition, however, both situations would be reported as $25,000 assets.

Disposition of Fixed Assets

If a fixed asset is used at least as long as the service life assigned to it in the depreciation calculation, its net accounting value is reduced to the estimated salvage value in the accounts. If the asset is retired from use and discarded, it's removed from the accounts by eliminating its original cost and accumulated depreciation.

Suppose equipment costing $21,000 is depreciated over sixty months with a zero salvage value. The equipment is used for seven years and then discarded. Just before the equipment is retired, it would be shown as having an original cost of $21,000 and accumulated depreciation of $21,000. Its net accounting value is $0, but it is still included in two different balance sheet accounts. When it's discarded, it is purged from the accounts by crediting the original cost by $21,000 and debiting accumulated depreciation by the same amount. Because this reduces the total equipment and accumulated depreciation amounts equally, it has no effect on the credit union's net amount of fixed assets.

Sometimes a fixed asset will be disposed of before it is depreciated down to its salvage value. Suppose a computer was purchased for $6,000 four years ago, assigned a salvage value of $0, and is being depreciated over sixty months. Depreciation of $100 is recorded each month, so after four years the accumulated depreciation is $4,800. The credit union decides the computer is no longer adequate and replaces it with a new machine. The old computer is sold for $500. The sales proceeds are less than the $1,200 net value the computer had in the credit union's accounts ($6,000 original cost less $4,800 accumulated depreciation). The credit union needs to record a loss on the sale of the computer, equal to the $700 difference between the net accounting value and the sales proceeds. This loss is recorded in a manner similar to an expense, at the same time the computer is removed from the accounts. The entire entry would be as follows:

In this chapter we've reviewed and expanded the concept of depreciation. As a credit union purchases fixed assets, the cost of those assets must be expensed on the income statement over a period of time. In this chapter we have only dealt with one method of depreciation—straight-line depreciation. While other methods of depreciation are allowed, most credit unions use straight-line depreciation. We move on to a discussion of accounting for liabilities and equity in the next chapter.

	Debit	Credit
Accumulated depreciation	$4,800	
Cash	$500	
Loss on sale of fixed asset	$700	
Equipment		$6,000

If the sale proceeds are larger than the fixed asset's net accounting value, the credit union would record the difference as a credit to "gain on sale" instead of a debit to the loss account.

Chapter 6 Accounting for Liabilities and Equity

As discussed in earlier chapters, *liabilities* represents one-third of the fundamental accounting equation: assets = liabilities + equity. Examples of liabilities include accounts payable, accrued dividends payable, payroll taxes payable, and accrued expenses.

What Is a Liability?

A liability arises from an event in the past that creates a future commitment. In credit union accounting, liabilities are obligations to perform certain actions in the future. The action could be to provide a service, but it's usually to transfer assets (most often cash). For example, when a credit union borrows money from its corporate credit union, it accepts an obligation to repay the full amount of the principal, plus interest, according to a set schedule.

Determinable, Estimated, and Contingent Liabilities

Certain types of liabilities can be precisely stated because the amount, the due date, and the person or entity to be paid are known. These are **determinable liabilities.** An example of this type of liability is a payable due to an office supplies company for loan forms in the amount of $100, due in thirty days.

Objectives

> Upon completion of this chapter, you will be able to
> 1. define liabilities, and understand their impact on your credit union's financial statements;
> 2. distinguish between a payable and an accrual;
> 3. record various accounting entries related to liability accounts;
> 4. understand the purpose of the regular reserve and undivided earnings accounts.

For some liabilities, however, the payee, amount, or due date may not be known. These are called **estimated liabilities.** Examples of these types of liabilities are property taxes payable and accrued audit fees. Since property tax rates are often determined during the year, the amount of this liability is uncertain when a business begins to accrue for the future expense at the beginning of the year. So, an accountant estimates the amount of tax based on past experience and expected changes in the property owned by the business. Both the amount and due date of accrued audit fees may be uncertain. Nevertheless, these liabilities are valid obligations of the credit union and need to be

---

A liability arises from an event in the past that creates a future commitment.

considered in the financial reporting process.

Contingent liabilities are potential obligations of a business. The liability depends on the occurrence or nonoccurrence of some future event. Examples of contingent liabilities include potential legal claims (such as lawsuits against the business) and guarantees (such as promises to repair or replace faulty goods sold). Further discussion of contingent liabilities is beyond the scope of this course.

Accounting for Specific Types of Liabilities

In this section, we'll discuss the entries required to properly account for three types of liability transactions, assuming you use an accrual accounting system:

1. accounts payable;
2. taxes payable;
3. accrued expenses.

Accounts Payable

Accounts payable are general trade obligations of a credit union incurred in the normal course of business for goods and services purchased on credit. Examples of accounts payable include billings received for monthly telephone and utility services, supplies purchased on credit, and amounts due for traveler's checks and money orders, and so on. In most cases of accounts payable, the supplier is the source of credit. If a business borrows money to purchase the item or service, the liability is usually recorded as a note or a mortgage payable.

Under accrual accounting, every transaction must be included in the period when the item was delivered or the expense was incurred. The credit union records the expense for the credit purchase as if the bill had been paid immediately. But it hasn't been. So the other half of the double entry is recorded in accounts payable as an obligation to transfer cash in a future period. Later, when the check is written for the item or service, the accounts payable entry recording that particular obligation is removed from the books.

Suppose Big Sky Federal Credit Union installs new phone system hardware on August 15, 20XX, but payment isn't due until a month later. The following journal entry records the purchase of the equipment:

	Debit	Credit
8/15/XX Fixed assets		
(telephone equipment)	4,000	
Accounts payable		4,000

Since this equipment is a fixed asset, it is also added to the depreciation calculation, as explained in the previous chapter.

When the invoice is paid on September 15, the following entry is recorded to recognize the fulfillment of the credit union's obligation:

	Debit	Credit
9/15/XX Accounts payable	4,000	
Cash		4,000

Recording the transaction in this manner, in accordance with accrual accounting principles, provides Big Sky with accurate month-end financial information on August 31 since

Basic Accounting
ACCOUNTING FOR LIABILITIES AND EQUITY

1. the new asset is included in the asset section of the balance sheet;
2. depreciation expense is properly recorded for August 15–31;
3. the obligation to transfer cash is accurately reflected in the liabilities section of the balance sheet.

Accounts payable can often be recorded with the day-to-day transactions of a business, rather than with the end-of-period adjustments.

Determine journal entries for a variety of accounts payable transactions by completing activity 6.1.

Taxes Payable

Businesses with employees are required to withhold payroll taxes on their behalf and remit them to the appropriate government agency. These taxes generally relate to federal income tax, social security, Medicare, state taxes, and possibly city taxes. Employers are also required to match employees' social security and Medicare contributions.

To illustrate the accounting requirements for withholding taxes, assume Big Sky Federal Credit Union has two employees. For the pay period ended March 31, the following information is known:

Activity 6.1 Recording Accounts Payable

List the journal entries for the following transactions.

1. Received invoice from local newspaper for $780 for display advertising for past month; payment is due by December 15.

   _____

   _____

   _____

2. Purchase of a delivery truck for $15,000; paid $3,000 cash and financed the remainder with a three-year loan from ABC Credit Union.

   _____

   _____

   _____

Answers appear in appendix A.

65

ACCOUNTING FOR LIABILITIES AND EQUITY

	Gross Wages	Federal Income Tax	Social Security Tax	Medicare Tax	State Income Tax	Net Wages
Sue Brown	$1,250.00	$200.00	$75.30	$18.58	$75.00	$881.12
John Smith	800.00	128.00	48.06	12.02	35.00	576.92
Total	$2,050.00	$328.00	$123.36	$30.60	$110.00	$1,458.04

If paychecks are written on March 31, the following entry would record the distribution of the payroll:

		Debit	Credit
3/31/XX	Payroll expense	2,050.00	
	Cash		1,458.04
	Federal withholding payable		328.00
	Social security withholding payable		123.36
	Medicare withholding payable		30.60
	State withholding payable		110.00

Big Sky's responsibility for the employer portion of social security and Medicare tax is recorded in different accounts, but in much the same manner and for exactly the same amount as the employees' portion.

When the payroll taxes are remitted to the appropriate federal and state agencies, the two entries shown next are recorded. For the sake of simplicity, we'll show only the balances from the March 15–31 period. However, when it comes time to remit payroll taxes, the balances will probably include amounts from several pay periods. The social security and Medicare *withholding payable* amounts shown are the employee portion. The *tax payable* amounts are Big Sky's share.

Assuming one payment is made to remit state taxes and another payment covers all the other amounts owed, the two required entries would be as follows:

	Debit	Credit
Federal withholding payable	328.00	
Social security withholding payable	123.36	
Medicare withholding payable	30.60	
Social security tax payable	123.36	
Medicare tax payable	30.60	
Cash		635.92

	Debit	Credit
State withholding payable	110.00	
Cash		110.00

Accrued Expenses

We covered accrued expenses in an earlier chapter when we discussed adjusting entries. To review, accrued expense adjustments allow you to record expenses in the proper accounting period, even though payment is not required at that time. Accounts payable also records liabilities that aren't due before the end of the period, but accrued expenses don't usually record the cost of items or services supplied on credit. Some of the types of accrued expenses credit unions encounter include:

- accrued payroll expense;

- accrued property taxes;
- accrued pension expense;
- accrued dividends;
- accrued audit fees.

The portion of these items incurred in each accounting period is recorded as an adjustment to an expense account and a liability account. Later, when payment is made, the liability is removed from the books.

Property tax is a good example. It is usually paid at the end of the year, yet one-twelfth of the tax liability is incurred during each month and is recorded at the end of each month as an expense even though no tax payment has been made. The accounting entry for the expense is offset by an equal increase in the accrued property tax account, which is a liability account. The balance in the accrual account builds up over the months. When the tax is paid in December or January, the balance drops and the accruals begin again in January for the next year.

The balance sheet and income statement show the business's true financial situation for a period only if the appropriate adjustments are made. Even businesses that don't use the full accrual method of accounting may accrue for certain expenses to make their financial statements more meaningful.

The accounting entries for most accrued expenses parallel the entries necessary for accrued payroll expense. We used a simple payroll example to illustrate the entries in an earlier chapter. Let's review those entries using a more realistic payroll example.

Suppose Big Sky Federal Credit Union wrote checks for the March 15–31 pay period on April 5 instead of March 31. The payroll expense must still be recorded for the month of March, but instead of dividing the matching entries among cash and taxes payable accounts, the entire amount of the matching entry is simply recorded as a liability, using an adjustment for March 31.

		Debit	Credit
3/31/XX	Payroll expense	2,050	
	Accrued payroll		2,050

The $2,050 payroll liability includes amounts owed to the employees, plus amounts withheld from the employees to be paid to government agencies on their behalf. However, it doesn't include amounts the credit union will pay out of its own pocket for taxes, so a second entry is required to accrue for those expenses.

		Debit	Credit
3/31/XX	Social security tax expense	$123.36	
	Medicare tax expense	30.60	
	Accrued taxes payable		153.96

When paychecks are written on April 5, the liability represented by the balance in the accrued payroll account has been fulfilled, so it is removed from the books.

Basic Accounting
ACCOUNTING FOR LIABILITIES AND EQUITY

		Debit	Credit
4/5/XX	Accrued payroll	2,050.00	
	Cash		1,458.04
	Federal withholding payable		328.00
	Social security withholding payable		123.36
	Medicare withholding payable		30.60
	State withholding payable		110.00

When the taxes are remitted, the payables are debited and the cash credited for the credit union's own tax expense and the amount withheld on behalf of the employees.

Summarize your understanding of accounting for accrued expenses in activity 6.2.

Financial Statement Presentation of Liabilities

On the balance sheets we've shown so far, we have listed all the liabilities. However, liabilities are often presented on a business's balance sheet in two major categories—current liabilities and long-term liabilities. A current liability is defined as an obligation that must be paid within one year. Conversely, a long-term liability is an obligation that extends beyond one year. Most businesses report current versus long-term liabilities (and assets) with a cutoff at one

---

Activity 6.2 Understanding Accrued Expenses

1. What is the purpose of accruing expenses?

   _____
   _____
   _____
   _____

2. What expenses are accrued in your credit union's accounting process?

   _____
   _____
   _____
   _____

3. What financial statement shows an accrued expense?

   _____

Basic Accounting
ACCOUNTING FOR LIABILITIES AND EQUITY

year, and credit unions often report considerably more detail about the maturities of their loans and shares. This information can be very useful for managers and directors in planning for future cash flows and the effect of changing interest rates on the credit union's interest income and dividend expenses.

The liability section of a credit union's statement of financial condition could appear as illustrated here:

Note: Though you won't see it in any of the examples in this course, each long-term liability is normally considered to have both a current portion and a long-term portion. The current portion is the amount that will come due in the current year. The long-term portion is all amounts that come due next year and after.

Credit Union Equity

As stated earlier, the equity section of the balance sheet of

---

Big Sky Federal Credit Union
(Partial) Statement of Financial Condition
March 31, 20XX

(dollars rounded off to whole numbers)

Current Liabilities
Accounts payable	$4,000	
Federal withholding payable	328	
Social security withholding payable	123	
Medicare withholding payable	31	
State withholding payable	110	
Total current liabilities		$4,592

Long-Term Liabilities
Mortgage payable	500,000	
Notes payable	250,000	
Total long-term liabilities		750,000

Total Liabilities — $754,592

most businesses reflects the portion of total assets not claimed by creditors. For a credit union, it reflects the portion of total assets not claimed by creditors or members. Thus, the balance sheet equation for credit unions is written this way:

Assets = Liabilities + Shares + Equity

The equity of a credit union is made up of undivided earnings and reserves.

Undivided Earnings

Undivided earnings are the net income of the current and prior periods that have not been transferred to regular reserves.

Regular Reserves

Regular reserves are part of the accumulated earnings of a credit union that have been earmarked to protect the credit union from loss. The amount that must be set aside in regular reserves is determined by regulation, as described next. Once earnings have been transferred to the regular reserve, they cannot be used to pay dividends and can only be used to absorb losses under limited circumstances. The regulation states:

> If a credit union's total net worth, defined as the sum of regular reserves and undivided earnings, falls below 7 percent of its assets, the credit union is required to build up its net worth. The increase must be equal to at least 0.1 percent of its assets per quarter, until the net worth reaches 7 percent of total assets. The minimum amount of new net worth (0.1 percent of assets per quarter) must be transferred to the regular reserve account.

For example, suppose a credit union had $100 million in total assets on June 30. It also had undivided earnings of $5 million and regular reserves of $1 million on that date, for total net worth of $6 million. Because the net worth is less than 7 percent of total assets, the credit union must add at least 0.1 percent of assets to net worth during the next quarter and transfer that amount to its regular reserves account. In other words, the credit union needs to earn net income of at least $100,000 during the July–September period and must also transfer at least that amount to the regular reserve account.

This system has two effects. First, it requires the credit union to build up its total equity (regular reserves and undivided earnings), thus making the credit union better able to absorb future losses without failing or needing external assistance. Second, by transferring funds from undivided earnings to regular reserves, that amount is made unavailable for dividend payments to members and thus becomes a relatively permanent base of equity for the credit union.

For credit unions affected by the regulation, the final closing entry is to transfer the required amount from undivided earnings to regular reserves, by debiting undivided earnings and crediting regular reserves.

Accounting for Credit Union Equity

Let's quickly review the entire closing process that transfers net income to the undivided earnings account and records the transfer to regular reserves. The credit union is shown in figure 6.1.

Begin by closing the income accounts with the following journal entry:

	Debit	Credit
12/31/XX Interest on loans	450,000	
Investment income	200,000	
Income summary		650,000

Close the expenses to the income summary account.

	Debit	Credit
12/31/XX Income summary	443,000	
Salaries		200,000
Rent expense		24,000
Utilities expense		6,000
Stationery and supplies expense		8,000
Insurance expense		10,000
Depreciation expense		20,000
Dividends expense		175,000

The balance in the income summary account—the net income for the year—is $207,000.

Income Summary	
	650,000
443,000	
	207,000

Close out the income summary account.

	Debit	Credit
12/31/XX Income summary	207,000	
Undivided earnings		207,000

Finally, record the transfer to regular reserves. While Riverside Credit Union would not be required by regulation to make a transfer, suppose the board of directors elects to make a voluntary transfer of $6,000 to regular reserves. This amount would be credited to the regular reserve and debited to undivided earnings.

	Debit	Credit
12/31/XX Undivided earnings	6,000	
Regular reserve		6,000

Figure 6.1 Adjusted Trial Balance

Riverside Credit Union
Adjusted Trial Balance
December 31, 20XX

	Debit	Credit
Interest on loans		$450,000
Investment income		$200,000
Salaries	$200,000	
Rent expense	24,000	
Utilities expense	6,000	
Stationery and supplies expense	8,000	
Insurance expense	10,000	
Depreciation expense	20,000	
Dividends expense	175,000	
Loans to members	4,000,000	
Cash	400,000	
Investments	1,000,000	
Furniture and equipment	200,000	
Accumulated depreciation, furniture and equipment		50,000
Accounts payable		5,000
Regular shares		3,600,000
Regular reserves		200,000
Undivided earnings		1,538,000
	$6,043,000	$6,043,000

ACCOUNTING FOR LIABILITIES AND EQUITY

In this chapter we've discussed two components of the balance sheet—liabilities and equity. In the next chapter, we wrap our discussion of basic accounting by looking at special journals and subsidiary ledgers.

Chapter 7 Special Journals and Subsidiary Ledgers

Accounting information is essential to the efficient management of your credit union. Within a credit union—or any other business organization—accounting information is produced by a system. The elements of the system include business papers, journals, ledgers, and other records. They also include the people who carry out the necessary procedures. Systems frequently include equipment such as computers and related software that has become integral to business data processing. Given all of the components, it's important that systems be designed to efficiently produce accurate information.

In this chapter we see how special journals and subsidiary ledgers assist in the development of an accurate and efficient accounting system. We also discuss how machines have relieved people of the burden of routine and repetitive tasks.

Reducing Writing and Posting Labor

We have seen in prior chapters that each transaction is recorded in a journal before it is posted to the general ledger. Thus far we have discussed only one type of journal—the general journal. While the general journal is very flexible in that it can record any type of transaction, it's not very efficient.

Objectives

Upon completion of this chapter, you will be able to

1. **identify special journals and what types of transactions are recorded in each;**
2. **explain how special journals save time when posting to the general ledger;**
3. **explain the need for subsidiary ledgers.**

Shortcomings of the General Journal

When an entry is recorded in the general journal, it's necessary to write out an explanation of the transaction that is being recorded. This explanation is needed because of all the different types of transactions that can be recorded in the general journal. And once a transaction is journalized in the general journal, it must be posted individually to the general ledger. There's no way to efficiently group or summarize transactions in the general journal for posting to the general ledger. For these reasons, special journals have been developed to simplify the recording and posting of transactions.

Special Journals Used in Accounting

Businesses with a large number of similar transactions may use a special journal to improve the efficiency of recording and posting transactions. The advantage of using a special journal is usually twofold. First, since all transactions recorded in the special journal are similar, an explanation of each transaction is not needed. And second, instead of posting each transaction separately to the general ledger, similar transactions are grouped together and posted collectively rather than individually.

Special journals used by many different types of businesses include sales journals, purchases journals, cash receipts journals, and cash disbursements journals. Transactions not recorded in the special purpose journals must be recorded in the general journal. Thus, all firms must have a general journal, but special journals are optional.

Even though credit unions do not often use the four special journals mentioned next, we introduce them here to help you understand how special journals can improve the efficiency of the accounting process.

Transactions not recorded in the special purpose journals must be recorded in the general journal.

Sales Journal

The sales journal is to record credit sales. (Sales journals are usually found in firms making wholesale or retail sales; they would be used less frequently in a credit union.) In addition to the dollar amount, the sales journal would contain a column to record the date, invoice number, and the person or company to whom the sale was made. The total amount of credit sales would be added up and posted as a debit to accounts receivable and as a credit to sales at the end of each month. Figure 7.1 is an example of one page from a sales journal.

Purchases Journal

A purchases journal is used to record all credit purchases. The journal contains columns to record the date, the company from whom the purchase was made, and various columns to help you sort the different types of purchases (for example, merchandise, equipment, furniture, and fixtures). The purchases journal in figure 7.2 is set up for a retail store that buys merchandise and supplies on credit, but other categories could be used.

Sorting purchases at the time they're journalized makes posting easier. The entire month's credit purchases can be transferred to the ledger with just a few entries. At the end of each month, the dollar amounts in each column would be added and posted to the general ledger. A single debit would be posted to the expense or asset account represented by each column, and a single credit would be posted to accounts payable.

Basic Accounting
SPECIAL JOURNALS AND SUBSIDIARY LEDGERS

Figure 7.1 Sales Journal

		SALES JOURNAL			PAGE 3
DATE	ACCOUNT DEBITED		INVOICE NUMBER	P.R.	AMOUNT

Figure 7.2 Purchases Journal

		PURCHASES JOURNAL						PAGE 3
DATE	ACCOUNT CREDITED	DATE OF INVOICE	TERMS	P.R.	ACCOUNTS PAYABLE CREDIT	MERCHANDISE DEBIT	STORE SUPPLIES DEBIT	OFFICE SUPPLIES DEBIT

Basic Accounting
SPECIAL JOURNALS AND SUBSIDIARY LEDGERS

Figure 7.3 Cash Receipts Journal

		CASH RECEIPTS JOURNAL						PAGE 3
DATE	ACCOUNT CREDITED	EXPLANATION	P.R.	OTHER ACCOUNTS CREDIT	ACCOUNTS RECEIVABLE CREDIT	SALES CREDIT	SALES DISCOUNTS DEBIT	CASH DEBIT

Figure 7.4 Cash Disbursements Journal

		CASH DISBURSEMENTS JOURNAL							PAGE 3
DATE	CH. NO.	PAYEE	ACCOUNT DEBITED	P.R.	OTHER ACCOUNTS DEBIT	ACCOUNTS PAYABLE DEBIT	PURCHASES DISCOUNTS CREDIT	CASH CREDIT	

Cash Receipts Journal

The cash receipts journal can be used to record cash that is collected by a business. In addition to a column to record the amount of cash collected, a separate column would be used to record the various sources of cash (for example, daily cash sales, cash received from customers on their accounts, or cash from miscellaneous sources). At the end of the month, cash would be debited for the total cash collected, and credits would be entered into the general ledger for the total of each source of cash.

The cash receipts journal in figure 7.3 has a column labeled "Other Accounts Credit." This column can be used to record cash collected for items other than accounts receivable and sales. Thus, the cash receipts journal illustrated could be used for transactions such as the sale of used office equipment for cash.

Cash Disbursements Journal

The cash disbursements journal is used to record each payment of cash from a checking account. This journal is similar to a check register in that it has a column for date, check number, page, and dollar amount. Unlike a check register, however, the cash disbursements journal helps you sort payments for more efficient posting. Hence, the cash disbursements journal also contains columns to record the type of payment being made. These columns normally include accounts payable, frequently used expense accounts, and other miscellaneous expenditures.

The cash disbursements journal in figure 7.4 has only two columns for debits, one to record payments on credit purchases and one to handle all other cash disbursements. At the end of the month, the columns in the cash disbursements journal would be footed (added up) and posted to the general ledger. The other accounts in both the cash receipts journal and the cash disbursements journal would not be posted in total but rather posted to a number of different accounts.

Each of these journals groups similar transactions and, therefore, the accountant can post monthly totals to the general ledger rather than individual transactions.

Types of Credit Union Transactions

Most industries choose to record their business transactions in a number of special journals such as the ones we've listed. Credit unions, however, have unique types of transactions. Most of the transactions of a credit union are member-related. These transactions deal with the exchange of cash and the balances of members' accounts. Due to their unique types of transactions, credit unions have developed a special journal that combines all of the journals into one book. The special journal used by credit unions is the journal and cash record (JCR) mentioned earlier when we first introduced the general journal. The JCR is explained more fully in the next course in this series, *Accounting for Credit Unions* (V310).

Summarize your understanding of the various special journals that are used in many accounting systems. Complete activity 7.1.

Credit unions have developed a special journal that combines all of the journals into one book.

Basic Accounting

SPECIAL JOURNALS AND SUBSIDIARY LEDGERS

Activity 7.1 Understanding Special Journals

1. What is the purpose of a special journal?

   _____
   _____
   _____
   _____

2. What type of business would most likely use the following kinds of special journals?
   Sales journal _____
   Purchases journal _____
   Cash receipts journal _____
   Cash disbursements journal _____

3. What special journals are used in your credit union's accounting system?

   _____
   _____
   _____

Subsidiary Ledgers

As discussed in chapter 2, the general ledger of a business consists of a loose-leaf book with a separate page for each account. To keep the size of the general ledger manageable, some accounts in the general ledger do not contain all the detail of the account but rather only the total. Such accounts are referred to as control accounts. An example of a control account in a credit union is member shares. The member shares account on the balance sheet doesn't tell us the balance each member has in his or her account. Because this information is critical, every credit union maintains a subsidiary ledger that contains the detail of each member's account. Periodically, the individual balances in the subsidiary ledger must be totaled and reconciled with the control account in the general ledger. The subsidiary ledger used by a credit union is called an individual share and loan ledger. This ledger is also explained more fully in the next course.

Businesses other than credit unions also use subsidiary ledgers to move the details of an account out of the general ledger. The subsidiary ledger most common to all types of businesses is the fixed-asset ledger.

Fixed-Asset Ledger

The fixed-asset ledger consists of a ledger sheet or card for each asset purchased by a business. The ledger sheet contains the detailed information needed for each individual item. Figure 7.5 shows three ledger cards for a credit union. Note that each ledger card has a description of the asset, purchase price, date of purchase, method of depreciation, location where the asset is kept, and detailed depreciation information.

The information contained in the fixed-asset subsidiary ledger is required for insurance purposes as well as for good financial management. To keep the fixed-asset subsidiary records at a manageable level, credit unions should establish a minimum amount at which to record fixed assets (usually $500–$1,000 depending on the credit union's size). If fixed-asset purchases fall below this level, they should be expensed.

Examine your credit union's fixed-asset ledger and complete activity 7.2.

Other Ledgers

Two other commonly used subsidiary ledgers are the accounts receivable ledger and the accounts payable ledger.

The accounts receivable ledger keeps detailed records on how much each customer owes a business. Since this information needs to be current, the accounts receivable ledger is posted daily. At the end of each month, when the special journals are posted to the general ledger, the total of the accounts receivable from each customer should equal the total accounts receivable in the general ledger. Every business that uses an accounts receivable ledger should require it to be reconciled to the general ledger every month.

The accounts payable ledger keeps detailed records on how much a business owes each of its suppliers. The accounts payable ledger should be updated daily in order to know the amount owed to each vendor. As with the accounts receivable ledger, a monthly reconciliation should be performed to ensure the control account in the general ledger is supported by the detail in the subsidiary ledger.

Basic Accounting
SPECIAL JOURNALS AND SUBSIDIARY LEDGERS

Figure 7.5 Furniture and Equipment Ledgers

Our Federal Credit Union
FURNITURE AND EQUIPMENT LEDGER

Description of item __Safe__ Stock number __774-1__
Depreciation schedule __Ten (10) Year Life: $30 Per Quarterly Period__
  Method: Straight Line Depreciation
Date purchased __2-1-X0__ Purchase price $ __1,200.00__ Date authorized __1-15-X0__
Date sold _____ Sales price $ _____ Date authorized _____
Where located __Manager's Office__

Date	Explanation	Debit	Credit	Balance
2-1-X0	Purchased safe	$1,200.00		$1,200.00
3-31-X0	Depreciation for 2 months		$20.00	$1,180.00
6-30-X0	Depreciation for 3 months		$30.00	$1,150.00
9-30-X0	Depreciation for 3 months		$30.00	$1,120.00
12-31-X0	Depreciation for 3 months		$30.00	$1,090.00

Our Federal Credit Union
FURNITURE AND EQUIPMENT LEDGER

Description of item __Executive Desk__ Stock number __774-2__
Depreciation schedule __Five (5) Year Life: $12.00 Per Quarterly Period__
  Method: Straight Line Depreciation
Date purchased __9-1-X9__ Purchase price $ __240.00__ Date authorized __6-30-X9__
Date sold _____ Sales price $ _____ Date authorized _____
Where located __Manager's Office__

Date	Explanation	Debit	Credit	Balance
9-1-X9	Purchased desk	$240.00		$240.00
9-30-X9	Depreciation for 1 month		$4.00	$236.00
12-31-X9	Depreciation for 3 months		$12.00	$224.00
3-31-X0	Depreciation for 3 months		$12.00	$212.00
6-30-X0	Depreciation for 3 months		$12.00	$200.00
9-30-X0	Depreciation for 3 months		$12.00	$188.00
12-31-X0	Depreciation for 3 months		$12.00	$176.00

Our Federal Credit Union
FURNITURE AND EQUIPMENT LEDGER

Description of item __Calculator__ Stock number __774-3__
Depreciation schedule __Five (5) Year Life: $6.00 Per Quarterly Period__
  Method: Straight Line Depreciation
Date purchased __3-1-X0__ Purchase price $ __120.00__ Date authorized __2-28-X0__
Date sold _____ Sales price $ _____ Date authorized _____
Where located __Loan Officer's Office__

Date	Explanation	Debit	Credit	Balance
3-1-X0	Purchased calculator	$120.00		$120
3-31-X0	Depreciation for 1 month		$2.00	$118
6-30-X0	Depreciation for 3 months		$6.00	$112
9-30-X0	Depreciation for 3 months		$6.00	$106
12-31-X0	Depreciation for 3 months		$6.00	$100

Activity 7.2 Examining the Fixed-Asset Ledger

1. Compare your credit union's fixed-asset ledger to the one shown in figure 7.5. Is the information the same? If not, what information is different?

2. What is the minimum cost of an asset recorded in your credit union's fixed-asset ledger?

3. Why should a business keep a fixed-asset ledger?

Computerized Systems

Many credit unions today have computerized some, if not all, of their accounting records. When using a computerized system, the journals and subsidiary ledgers do not take the same form as the ones presented in this course, which are designed for a manual system. Once you have a good understanding of how a manual system works, you will be able to adapt to a computerized system. In a computerized system, journals take the form of transaction registers, and subsidiary ledgers may be contained within the general ledger. However, the basic concept of journals and ledgers still exists. In the next course we discuss a special journal and a subsidiary ledger that are unique to credit union accounting.

Wrap-Up

This course has given you a general understanding of accounting. We began with the introduction of two basic financial statements—the income statement and the balance sheet.

The balance sheet equation illustrated how these statements are related.

Our study of the system of debits and credits enhanced our understanding of how transactions are actually recorded. The use of journals and ledgers provides us with the procedures accountants use to record and summarize transactions. The accrual basis of accounting was introduced because it accurately reflects the financial condition of a business.

Accrual accounting requires that revenues be recorded when earned, and not necessarily when cash is received. By the same reasoning, accrual accounting requires expenses to be recorded when incurred, and not necessarily when paid. The study of accrual accounting led us to the need for adjusting entries at the end of each accounting period. The trial balance worksheet was introduced as a tool used by accountants to facilitate the adjusting process.

Once the financial statements are prepared, a business must close out its revenue and expense accounts to a zero balance before it is ready to begin the accounting process for the next period. The closing process completes the accounting cycle of the business.

After going through the mechanics of the accounting cycle, we expanded our study of the balance sheet accounts. The concept of depreciation was introduced, and the straight-line method of depreciation was illustrated along with the financial statement presentation of fixed assets.

The second type of balance sheet account discussed was liabilities. A distinction was made between liabilities that are payables and those that are accrued expenses. Financial statement presentation was also addressed with an illustration of how current liabilities are separated from long-term liabilities on the balance sheet.

Equity was the final balance sheet category discussed. The unique equity accounts of a credit union—regular reserves and undivided earnings—were introduced and explained.

To complete this introductory course, we discussed special journals and ledgers used by accountants. While those discussed are not those necessarily used by a credit union, they do provide the foundation for the next course in this series, which introduces the journals and ledgers used by a credit union with a manual accounting system. An understanding of a manual system will lead to an understanding of the computerized systems used by most credit unions today. Computerized accounting systems greatly reduce the time required to process the transactions and produce the financial reports described in these courses.

Appendix A Answers to Activities

Activity 1.1 Understanding the Bookkeeping Process

1. c
2. a
3. g
4. e
5. b
6. f
7. d

Activity 1.3 Reviewing Financial Statements

1. B
2. B
3. I
4. B
5. I
6. I
7. B
8. I
9. B
10. B

Activity 2.1 Maintaining the Balance Sheet Equation

Debits	
Cash (net)	$ 1,300
Furniture and equipment	4,000
Investments	9,000
Rent	100
Total	$14,400

Credits	
Notes payable	$ 3,500
Member shares	10,000
Investment income	900
Total	$14,400

Basic Accounting
ANSWERS TO ACTIVITIES

Activity 2.2 Posting to a Ledger

General Ledger for J.C. Carpentry

Carpentry Services — Account No. 110

Date	Explanation	P/R	Debit	Credit	Balance
07/07/xx		J1		2,750	(2,750)

Salaries — Account No. 210

Date	Explanation	P/R	Debit	Credit	Balance
07/03/xx		J1	2,400		2,400

Rent — Account No. 220

Date	Explanation	P/R	Debit	Credit	Balance
07/01/xx		J1	1,000		1,000

Utilities — Account No. 230

Date	Explanation	P/R	Debit	Credit	Balance
07/09/xx		J1	457		457

Supplies — Account No. 240

Date	Explanation	P/R	Debit	Credit	Balance
07/09/xx		J1	100		100

Cash — Account No. 310

Date	Explanation	P/R	Debit	Credit	Balance
07/01/xx		J1		1,000	(1,000)
07/05/xx		J1		2,400	(3,400)
07/07/xx		J1	3,215		(185)
07/09/xx		J1		457	(642)
07/10/xx		J1		500	(1,142)
07/15/xx		J1		100	(1,242)

Accounts Receivable — Account No. 320

Date	Explanation	P/R	Debit	Credit	Balance
07/07/xx		J1		3,215	(3,215)
07/07/xx		J1	2,750		(465)

Equipment — Account No. 330

Date	Explanation	P/R	Debit	Credit	Balance
07/10/xx		J1	3,000		3,000

Notes Payable — Account No. 410

Date	Explanation	P/R	Debit	Credit	Balance
07/10/xx		J1		2,500	(2,500)

Basic Accounting
ANSWERS TO ACTIVITIES

Activity 2.3 Preparing a Trial Balance

J.C. Carpentry
Trial Balance
July 15, 20XX

	Debit	Credit
Carpentry services		2,750
Salaries	2,400	
Rent	1,000	
Utilities	457	
Supplies	100	
Cash	(1,242)	
Accounts receivable	(465)	
Equipment	3,000	
Notes payable		2,500
Total	5,250	5,250

Activity 4.1 Preparing Financial Statements

1. F
2. F
3. F
4. T
5. F
6. T

Activity 5.2 Calculating Depreciation

Office building depreciation expense = $555.56
Computer system depreciation expense = $1,166.67
Automobile depreciation expense = $291.67

Basic Accounting

ANSWERS TO ACTIVITIES

Activity 6.1 Recording Accounts Payable

			Debit	Credit
1. 11/20/XX	Advertising expense		780	
	Accounts payable			780
2. 12/15/XX	Fixed assets		15,000	
	Cash			3,000
	Notes payable			12,000

Appendix B Glossary

accounts payable Accounts representing purchases made or expenses incurred, for which payment is not made immediately but is delayed to some point—usually within a month of the expenditure.

accrual basis A method of accounting in which revenue is recognized in the accounting period in which it is earned, regardless of whether payment has been received.

amortization The process of allocating an amount across a span of time, apportioning it among units of time within the span.

asset Anything having monetary value that is owned by a person or an organization.

asset account One of three types of accounts that appear on a balance sheet, listing items such as receivables, merchandise, inventory, supplies, equipment, buildings, and land.

balance sheet A statement of financial position listing assets owned, liabilities owed, and the credit union's equity as of a specific date. It is sometimes called a *statement of financial condition.*

capital Represents *net worth* or *net value,* as well as ownership in an enterprise. Capital can be measured by the excess of assets over liabilities. In a narrower sense, credit union "capital" may refer only to institutional capital: reserves and undivided earnings. Also known as *equity.*

capitalized costs Costs of assets for which the benefits are obtained over more than one accounting period.

cash basis A method of accounting whereby sellers of products and services recognize revenue on the day that actual payment is received.

contingent liabilities Potential obligations that are dependent on future factors that may or may not materialize or on events that may or may not happen. Examples of contingent liabilities include potential legal claims and guarantees.

corporation A legal entity formed in a legally established process called incorporation; the owners and stockholders are legally separate and distinct from the corporation. Many corporations are investor-owned, for-profit corporations, but some, such as credit unions, are not-for-profit.

credit An amount entered on the right side. A credit increases liabilities, equity, and income. A credit decreases assets and expenses.

Basic Accounting
GLOSSARY

debit An amount entered on the left side. A debit increases assets and expenses. A debit decreases liabilities, equity, and income.

determinable liabilities Liabilities that can be precisely stated because the amount, the due date, and the person or entity to be paid are known, such as a payable due.

dividends Payments distributed to a cooperative's owners.

equity Total assets less total liabilities, also known as *capital, net worth,* or *net value.*

equity account One of the three types of accounts that appear on a balance sheet, representing the value of the owners' stake in the business. Equity equals total assets minus total liabilities. Credit unions have two types of equity accounts—*reserves* and *undivided earnings.*

estimated liabilities Liabilities for which the payee, amount, or due date may not be known, such as property taxes payable and accrued audit fees.

expenses What is spent to acquire and use goods and services during operations.

fixed assets Relatively long-lived assets that are used to produce goods and services and/or other assets.

general ledger The book on file where all the accounts of a business are collected.

income The amount of cash or receivables credit unions gain from interest on loans and investments, and fees charged for services.

income statement A financial statement related to a specific period of time, rather than one point in time, showing whether an entity has gained financially or lost over the specified period.

liabilities Claims made by creditors, employees, and others on a business's assets—usually specified amounts of cash—in exchange for services performed or goods provided for purposes of running a business.

liability account One of the three types of accounts that appear on a balance sheet showing the debts and obligations owed to others, such as accounts payable, wages payable, taxes payable, notes payable, and mortgages payable.

line item An entry as it appears on a separate line on a financial statement.

net income The difference between total revenue and total expenses for the period covered by a particular income statement. Also known as *margin.*

partnership Two or more people owning and operating a business under a formal agreement. In a partnership, owners share equally in the responsibilities, liabilities, and profits of the business unless stated otherwise in the articles of partnership and pay taxes as individuals.

receivable A debt owned to the business that will be paid within a relatively short period of time.

regular reserves Reserves required by law to protect credit union members from potential losses.

share certificate account An account in which deposits, if held for a minimum period of time in the account, earn dividends at a specified rate that is usually higher than the rate for share and share draft accounts.

share draft account An account holding shares on which members can withdraw money by means of drafts.

sole proprietorship An unincorporated business owned and controlled by one person who is personally responsible for all obligations or liabilities of the business. Sole proprietors are treated as an individual account and may open interest-bearing accounts, unlike corporations.

statement of financial condition A statement of financial position listing assets owned, liabilities owed, and the credit union's equity as of a specific date. Also called a *balance sheet*.

statutory reserves Earnings required to be set aside by law and held in a reserve account designed to protect members from potential loan losses.

undivided earnings The combined earnings of the credit union (revenue left over after operating expenses) that have not been put into the regular reserves account.

variance The dollar difference between current actual results and budgeted results.

Appendix C Resources

Learning Opportunities from CUNA's Center for Professional Development

The CUNA Center for Professional Development (CPD) designs training materials and schools specific to credit unions. CPD resources are available to help develop credit union careers in all areas of operations.

For more information about CPD training for credit unions, you can

- browse the training resources listed below for options that fit your needs, then
- call your state league education director, or
- call CUNA Customer Service at (800)356-8010, ext. 4157, or
- explore the "Training & Education" section at CUNA's web site, *www.cuna.org*.

Books

The Center for Professional Development publishes a number of books that serve as references and resources for specific areas and topics. Any of the books listed here can be ordered by calling CUNA Customer Service at (800)356-8010, ext. 4157, or by using the form in the back of this book. Internet users can obtain information and order online by visiting the "Training & Education" section at CUNA's web site, *www.cuna.org*.

Credit Union Investment Guidelines, fourth edition

Here's a guide that treats managing investments as a process, not an event. Author Brian Hague, economist and CEO of Corporate Network Brokerage Services, says that credit unions should avoid simply reacting to attractive investment opportunities. *Credit Union Investment Guidelines* maps out the complete investment process. It explains how to execute a trade in the proper context of the management process. Its chapters give you information on

- sound investment policies;
- risk and return policies;
- yield curve;
- recent changes to NCUA's rules and Regulations, Part 703;
- investment objectives;
- asset allocation;
- portfolio monitoring and rebalancing;
- portfolio management and strategies.

Credit Union Investment Guidelines also includes an investment policy checklist and a glossary of investment terms. #21142-M2, 194 pages, $54.95

Economics for Credit Union Professionals

This comprehensive book uses credit union examples to explain the key concepts of modern economics in nontechnical language. *Economics for Credit Union Professionals* includes information on

- money and its functions;
- money markets in operation;
- money supply and its effect on interest rates;
- reserve requirements;
- discount policy;
- supply and demand;

- price elasticity and how it affects pricing;
- government regulations;
- prices and employment;
- the international monetary system;
- current economic problems.

Economics for Credit Union Professionals provides question-and-answer review sections to help readers evaluate their comprehension. #23398-M2, 207 pages, $59.95

Managing Credit Union Finance

Effective credit union leadership requires a sound understanding of financial management principles. Analysis and planning make the difference between lending and simply running programs. *Managing Credit Union Finance* is a valuable resource for management at all levels on topics necessary for credit union success. This book examines and reviews

- the credit union financial management process;
- financial statement analysis;
- capitalization;
- pricing member services;
- interest-rate risk and investments;
- managing liquidity;
- lending considerations;
- credit union service organizations;
- the asset-liability management policy;
- the annual business plan;
- internal controls.

Managing Credit Union Finance uses credit union examples to illustrate the practical application of financial management concepts. #23497-M2, 177 pages, $59.95

The Power of Business Ethics: Credit Union Ideals in the Real World

The Power of Business Ethics, by Dick Radtke, takes on the 150-year history of cooperative credit and shows how our values are prized in today's economic environment. Credit unions have a huge advantage in marketing our cooperative difference, the advantage of being the one to "ride the white horse" in the marketplace. This book provokes readers to understand our fascinating, unique story and build on it for even greater success. Included are

- a unique perspective that shows why credit unions are a special breed;
- ethical standards for employers;
- ethical standards for employees;
- ethics and the member;
- ethics and the community;
- communicating ethical standards.

Examples to inspire discussion and debate are included, as well as a glossary and lists of selected references and resources. It provides tools and suggestions for building consensus on ethics within the credit union and for demonstrating ethics and values to members and the public. #23166-M2, 123 pages, $29.95

Basic Accounting
RESOURCES

STAR (Staff Training and Recognition)
The STAR program focuses on the knowledge and skill needs of frontline staff. Staff members can study alone, or the credit union can structure a training program to help them build the skills they need to serve members. STAR courses and exams are available in a printed version, and most are available online.

To order the print versions of STAR courses, contact your state league representative. Credit unions in Arizona, California, and Nevada can order directly from CUNA Customer Service by calling (800)356-8010, ext. 4157. Internet users can learn more about these books and online training opportunities by visiting the "Training & Education" section at CUNA's web site, *www.cuna.org*.

Relevant STAR courses include:

S310 Accounting for Credit Unions
This course remains focused on the basic accounting cycle introduced in course *S300 Basic Accounting,* while looking much more closely at situations and practices specific to credit unions. It describes the accounts most commonly used by federal and state-chartered credit unions; source documents; journal and cash records; subsidiary ledgers; the general ledger; internal control; accounting for cash, loans, and member shares; reserves and undivided earnings; and financial statements, income statements, and balance sheets and includes a discussion of current trends in credit union accounting.

S320 Credit Union Financial Analysis
One of the most difficult challenges credit unions face is balancing risk and return. At the end of the year, a credit union's financial statements will reflect the wisdom, skill, and luck of those who manage that balance. The objective of this course is to help credit union staff understand financial analysis—the techniques and formats managers use to select meaningful information, do the proper analysis, and balance risk and return. Chapters cover the concerns and approaches used by the financial analyst, analysis of the balance sheet and the income statement, loan analysis, liquidity and interest-rate spreads, trend analysis, financial comparison, and NCUA's CAMEL rating system.

S1200 Financial Management Made Easy I: Financial Statements and Budgeting
The success or failure of any business pivots on the quality of its management, which in turn depends on accurate recordkeeping. *Financial Management Made Easy I: Financial Statements and Budgeting* present the tools of financial management. It focuses on financial statements and ratios, asset-liability management, spread analysis, the effects of interest-rate changes, budget planning, and budget reports. It's an easy-to-read introduction to the principles of credit union financial decision making. Together with *S1210 Financial Management Made Easy II: Sources and Uses of Money,* this course serves as a guide for staff trainees with different levels of financial knowledge.

S1210 Financial Management Made Easy II: Sources and Uses of Money
It's important for staff to understand the financial workings of the credit union. By understanding why management makes certain financial decisions, staff will accept changes in the workplace, assist the credit union in reaching its goals, deal more effectively with members, and supply valuable input to management. *Financial Management Made Easy II: Sources and Uses of Money* focuses on pricing credit union services, loan risk and financial management, capitalization, investments, liquidity, and cash flow. It is written with the assumption that staff trainees are familiar with

Basic Accounting
RESOURCES

the material presented in course S1200 *Financial Management Made Easy I: Financial Statements and Budgeting.* Each chapter in both courses includes a glossary of key words and a summary of key points. A complete glossary of financial terms appears at the end of each course.

MERIT (Management Enrichment Training)

The MERIT program helps credit union employees develop the skills needed for management success. It includes courses on leadership, communication, employee relations, conflict management, team building, marketing, lending, and strategic management. Completion of MERIT courses creates opportunities to move up the career ladder and shows upper management a commitment to a credit union career. MERIT courses and exams are available in a printed version, and most are available online.

To order the print versions of MERIT courses, contact your state league representative. Credit unions in Arizona, California, and Nevada can order directly from CUNA Customer Service by calling (800)356-8010, ext. 4157. Internet users can learn more about these books and online training opportunities by visiting the "Training & Education" section at CUNA's web site, *www.cuna.org*.

Relevant MERIT courses include:

M17 Credit Union Financial Management for Nonfinancial Executives
This course presents an efficient overview of credit union financial operations. This easy-to-understand course includes information on capital adequacy, asset-liability management, cash-flow forecasting, spread analysis, and ratio analysis. It also includes information about balance sheets, income statements, and risk management.

M18 Asset-Liability Management for Executives
With regulations such as Part 703 requiring increased asset-liability management expertise, this is a timely read. This course provides the tools to determine credit, liquidity, and interest-rate risk—and the means to apply these tools. You will learn how to track credit union performance. Nonfinancial staff should complete course M17 before beginning this course.

M31 Budgeting and Accounting for Nonaccounting Managers
This course helps credit union personnel better understand accounting. The course takes students step by step through the basic accounting process and then fills in details of accounting systems, asset accounting, liabilities, shares and reserves, budgeting, and planning.

M33 Financial Analysis Tools for Decision Making
This course shows effective ways for nonfinancial managers to use appropriate financial analysis tools to evaluate new products and services. You will discover the tools needed for making decisions with financial implications for your credit union.

CEP (Certified Executive Program)

The Certified Executive Program offers college-level courses that help those aspiring to credit union leadership develop management skills. CEP is designed for anyone whose goal is effective, strategic credit union leadership. It provides comprehensive, challenging education in operations and management areas. Professional designations that can be earned are the Certified Credit Union Executive (CCUE) designation and the Certified Financial Services Professional (CFSP) designation. Specialty certifications are available for financial management, marketing, human resources, compliance, and lending specialization. For more information call (800)356-9655, ext. 4123; e-mail *cunacep@cuna.coop;* or visit the "Training & Education" section at CUNA's web site, *www.cuna.org*.

RegTraC (Regulatory Training and Certification)

The Regulatory Training and Certification program is a comprehensive self-study source for up-to-date compliance information, written in plain English. The program offers two levels of certification: Level 1 is designed for noncompliance staff and anyone interested in a general discussion of the regulations. Level 2 is designed to meet the needs of staff directly responsible for credit union compliance and anyone interested in the specific requirements of the regulations. Lessons cover all major federal regulations that affect credit unions, as well as critical NCUA opinion letters. Material is regularly updated. For more information call (800)356-9655, ext. 4066, or visit the "Training & Education" section at CUNA's web site, *www.cuna.org*.

Schools and Conferences

Center for Professional Development (CPD) schools and conferences are in-depth and beyond the ordinary! Many of these weeklong programs offer participants the opportunity to earn continuing professional education credits in a choice of two exciting locations. For more information, or to register for these schools, call (800)356-9655, ext. 4249, or visit the "Training & Education" section at CUNA's web site, *www.cuna.org*.

Many of these programs can be taken in the comfort of your home or office by registering for CPD eSchools. These online schools provide a unique blended approach to learning that features live, real-time interactive instruction from industry experts, combined with self-paced web activities, group discussions, exercises, simulations, and case studies. CPD's eSchools provide the same learning objectives and return on your investment—the difference is in the delivery channel. For more information on eSchools, visit the "Training & Education" section at CUNA's web site, *www.cuna.org*; call (800)356-9655, ext. 4864; or e-mail *elearning@cuna.coop*.

Financial Management Schools: Part I

This school is available both on-site and online through the Virtual Classroom. Sessions cover

- the state of credit union financial management;
- an introduction to asset-liability management;
- financial planning;
- hands-on simulation modeling in asset-liability management;
- ration analysis;
- investment policy;
- budgeting.

Financial Management Schools: Part II

This school is available both on-site and online through the Virtual Classroom. Sessions cover

- a computer simulation case study introduction for those who didn't attend part I;
- the state of credit union financial management;
- pricing financial services;
- advanced asset-liability management: interest-rate risk assessment;
- hands-on simulation modeling in building a financial plan;
- managing core deposits;
- financial planning and budgeting;
- capital adequacy management and the financial planning case;
- portfolio management strategies;
- investment options to achieve financial goals and objectives.

Basic Accounting
RESOURCES

Web Sites

Users should review information found on these web sites for accuracy, completeness, and timeliness. Web publishers offer no warranties on the material they present.

www.bankrate.com Web site that contains rate comparisons and information on over 100 financial products including mortgages, credit cards, new and used automobile loans, money market accounts, certificates of deposit, checking and ATM fees, home equity loans, and online banking fees.

www.bloomberg.com Bloomberg Financial Markets offers financial news and columns from the personal finance magazine *Bloomberg Personal*.

www.cuna.org Web site for CUNA (Credit Union National Association), based in Washington, D.C. and Madison, Wisconsin. CUNA is the premier national trade association serving U.S. credit unions. This site contains links to consumer information, governmental affairs, regulations, products, technology, research, training, publications, conferences, press releases, and networking opportunities.

Cucenter.cuna.org Credit Union Executive Center is a dynamic new online information source for news, in-depth articles, peer sharing, and statistics on lending, technology, human resources, operations, finance, and more—the intelligence you need to serve your members and advance your career. (It is correct that there is no *www* in this address.)

www.cunamutual.com Official web site for CUNA Mutual Group, the leading financial services provider to credit unions and their members worldwide. More than 300 insurance, investment, and technological solutions are offered through strategic relationships and multiple service channels. Visit the the Products & Resources section to obtain compliance and easy-to-use forms and disclosures through Members' Enterprise.

www.ffiec.gov Web site for the Federal Financial Institutions Examination Council (FFIE). The council is a formal interagency body empowered to prescribe uniform principles, standards, and report forms for the federal examination of financial institutions by various national agencies. This site gives access to Home Mortgage Disclosure Act (HMDA) reporting information, updated reports and press releases from the FFIEC, information on handbooks and catalogs, enforcement actions and orders, online information systems, and many topics relevant to financial institutions.

www.harlandfinancialsolutions.com Web site for Harland Financial Solutions, Inc., a wholly owned subsidiary of the John H. Harland Company, one of the leading providers of technology to U.S. financial institutions. Harland Financial Solutions products include deposit and loan origination, platform, teller, call-center, mortgage, business intelligence, core processing, and customer relationship management systems.

www.ihsfinancial.com Web site for IHS Financial Products, now known as CCH Financial Products. This site contains a link to the credit union library, a comprehensive collection of compliance information created specifically for the unique needs of the credit union industry. Subscribers to this library have instant access to important documents such as the United States Code, state laws and regulations, Federal Register/USC Updates, Federal Reserve publications, NCUA publications, CUNA publications, and FFIEC publications.

www.irs.ustreas.gov Web site for the Internal Revenue Service's (IRS) online newspaper, *The Digital Daily.* It contains links to information on tax issues and regulations and has forms and publications in downloadable form.

www.moneycentral.msn.com Money, an online magazine, offers personal finance basics covering real estate, insurance, and taxes, as well as retirement.

www.myfico.com Web site provided by FairIsaac, the company that introduced credit scoring. Credit union members can order their FICO score and learn how to improve it at this site.

www.ncua.gov Web site for the National Credit Union Administration (NCUA). NCUA is an independent federal agency that supervises and insures 6,566 federal credit unions and 4,062 state-chartered credit unions. This site provides direct access to credit union data, updates on the actions of NCUA, links to federal government agencies, bylaws for federal credit unions, rules and regulations, regulatory alerts, the Federal Credit Union Act, current news, information on the Small Credit Union Program, and numerous links to credit union-related sites.

www.quicken.com The Quicken software company offers diverse financial information, including up-to-date summaries of the most common retirement plans and an online financial calculator.

Appendix D Test Questions

Answers to these test questions are to be marked on either the scannable answer sheet or competency test provided. Please do not mark answers in the text or return these pages to be graded. Photocopies of scannable answer sheets and competency tests will not be accepted. Original scannable answer sheets are to be returned to CUNA in the envelope provided. Original competency tests are to be returned to your league education department.

1. The three most common forms of business organizations (aside from government-run) are
   a. sole proprietorship, cooperative, partnership.
   b. cooperative, partnership, corporation.
   c. partnership, corporation, sole proprietorship.
   d. corporation, sole proprietorship, cooperative.

2. A credit union is a not-for-profit, cooperative
   a. sole proprietorship.
   b. partnership.
   c. government organization.
   d. corporation.

3. The equity of a credit union includes
   a. common stock.
   b. loans to members.
   c. savings accounts.
   d. regular reserves.

4. The income statement
   a. includes assets, liabilities, and equity.
   b. shows the financial condition of a business at a particular date.
   c. shows the net financial gain for a specific period of time.
   d. includes all the assets of the business.

Basic Accounting

TEST QUESTIONS

5. The balance sheet shows
   a. the financial condition of a business at a particular date.
   b. the financial condition of a business for a specific period of time.
   c. total revenues for the period covered.
   d. total expenses for the period covered.

6. The balance sheet equation is
   a. revenues = assets.
   b. assets = liabilities + equity.
   c. revenues – expenses = net income.
   d. expenses = liabilities.

7. The word *debit* comes from a Latin word meaning
   a. increase.
   b. left.
   c. decrease.
   d. right.

8. The following accounts are increased by debits:
   a. assets and liabilities
   b. assets and expenses
   c. liabilities and owner's equity
   d. expenses and owner's equity

9. The following accounts are increased by credits:
   a. income and expenses
   b. expenses and liabilities
   c. liabilities and income
   d. income and assets

10. A book of original entry is
    a. a journal.
    b. a general ledger.
    c. a subsidiary ledger.
    d. a ledger.

11. A listing of all accounts in the general ledger and their debit or credit balance is called
    a. a balance sheet.
    b. an income statement.
    c. a posting.
    d. a trial balance.

12. The method of accounting in which income is recognized when it is earned and expenses are recognized when they are incurred is called
    a. cash basis accounting.
    b. double-entry accounting.
    c. accrual basis accounting.
    d. single-entry accounting.

100

13. The adjusting entry to record investment income that has been earned but not received by the end of an accounting period is
    a. Dr. cash, Cr. investment income.
    b. Dr. accrued investment income, Cr. investment income.
    c. Dr. investment income, Cr. cash.
    d. Dr. cash, Cr. accrued investment income.

14. Payments made prior to receiving goods or services are called
    a. prepaid expenses.
    b. liabilities.
    c. depreciation.
    d. expenses.

15. The term used to allocate the cost of an expensive fixed asset over the period of time the asset will be used is called
    a. posting.
    b. prepayment.
    c. depreciation.
    d. cash basis accounting.

16. The process of recording all transactions in the general ledger from the journal is called
    a. journalizing.
    b. debiting.
    c. posting.
    d. adjusting.

17. The form that contains the correct period-end balance of every account in the general ledger is
    a. the income statement.
    b. the balance sheet.
    c. the statement of financial condition.
    d. the adjusted trial balance.

18. The first pair of money columns on a worksheet are used to record
    a. the income statement.
    b. the unadjusted trial balance.
    c. the balance sheet.
    d. the year-end adjustments.

19. The balance sheet of a credit union is often referred to as
    a. the statement of financial condition.
    b. the worksheet.
    c. the adjusted trial balance.
    d. the income statements.

Basic Accounting

TEST QUESTIONS

20. When closing the books of a credit union, the income summary account is closed to
    a. the revenue accounts.
    b. the expense accounts.
    c. the undivided earnings account.
    d. the worksheet.

21. Closing entries bring the following accounts to a zero balance
    a. assets and liabilities
    b. income and expenses
    c. income and owners equity
    d. assets and expenses

22. The cost of furniture and equipment should include
    a. purchase price.
    b. delivery charges.
    c. setup charges.
    d. all of the above

23. If a building is purchased for $600,000 and is depreciated over forty years using $0 salvage value, the monthly straight-line depreciation would be
    a. $15,000.
    b. $12,500.
    c. $1,250.
    d. $625.

24. If furniture is purchased for $12,248, is depreciated using straight-line depreciation over seven years, and has $2,000 salvage value, the monthly depreciation would be
    a. $1,020.
    b. $510.
    c. $146.
    d. $122.

25. The entry to record depreciation on a building is
    a. Dr. depreciation expense, Cr. buildings.
    b. Dr. accumulated depreciation—building, Cr. buildings.
    c. Dr. depreciation expense, Cr. accumulated depreciation.
    d. Dr. buildings, Cr. accumulated depreciation-building.

26. Liabilities that must be paid within one year are classified on the statement of financial condition as
    a. expenses.
    b. current liabilities.
    c. long-term liabilities.
    d. assets.

27. Most of the balance of a mortgage payable over the next fifteen years would be classified as
    a. a current asset.
    b. a current liability.
    c. a long-term liability.
    d. a long-term asset.

28. An expense that has been incurred but is not yet due or payable at the end of an accounting period is
    a. an accrued expense.
    b. an accounts payable.
    c. an asset.
    d. a long-term liability.

29. Allocations of undivided earnings of a credit union to protect members against losses are called
    a. assets.
    b. regular reserves.
    c. liabilities.
    d. expenses.

30. Undivided earnings is classified as
    a. an asset.
    b. a liability.
    c. a member share.
    d. an equity account.

31. The journal used to record sales on credit is
    a. the sales journal.
    b. the purchases journal.
    c. the cash receipts journal.
    d. the cash disbursement journal.

32. The journal used to record cash collected by a business is
    a. the sales journal.
    b. the cash receipts journal.
    c. the cash disbursements journal.
    d. the purchases journal.

33. The subsidiary ledger that keeps detailed records on how much each customer owes is called
    a. the fixed-asset ledger.
    b. the accounts receivable ledger.
    c. the general ledger.
    d. the accounts payable ledger.

34. The journal used to record all purchases on credit is
    a. the purchases journal.
    b. the cash receipts journal.
    c. the cash disbursements journal.
    d. the sales journal.

Basic Accounting

TEST QUESTIONS

35. The journal used to record cash payments from a checking account is
    a. the sales journal.
    b. the cash receipts journal.
    c. the purchases journal.
    d. the cash disbursements journal.

36. The subsidiary ledger that shows how much a business owes each of its suppliers is
    a. the accounts payable ledger.
    b. the fixed-asset ledger.
    c. the general ledger.
    d. the accounts receivable ledger.

37. The journal used to record year-end adjusting and closing entries is
    a. the cash receipts journal.
    b. the purchases journal.
    c. the sales journal.
    d. the general journal.

38. The subsidiary ledger that keeps detailed information on furniture and equipment is
    a. the general ledger.
    b. the accounts receivable ledger.
    c. the fixed-asset ledger.
    d. the accounts payable ledger.

39. The book of final entry to which postings are made from all the journals is
    a. the fixed-asset ledger.
    b. the accounts receivable ledger.
    c. the general ledger.
    d. the accounts payable ledger.

40. A credit union is a not-for-profit corporation that is owned by
    a. the federal government.
    b. its stockholder.
    c. the state government.
    d. its members.

Evaluation Questions

Please complete these evaluation questions after you have taken the test. Mark appropriate answers on the scannable answer sheet or competency test under numbers 41 through 44.

41. I am taking this course through
    a. correspondence.
    b. chapter/credit union study group.
    c. league sponsored conference or workshop.
    d. credit union in-house training program.

42. Overall, I feel this course was
    a. excellent.
    b. good.
    c. fair.
    d. poor.

43. This course was
    a. practical.
    b. interesting.
    c. irrelevant.
    d. boring.

44. The competency test was
    a. fair.
    b. clear.
    c. tricky.
    d. vague.

Index

(Page numbers shown in italic type refer to figures, tables or similar material.)

A

accounting
   accrual basis, 33–34, 82
   bookkeeping and, 5–8
   double-entry, 6, 17–18
   financial statements, 9–17 (*see also* financial statements)
   overview, 3–5
accounting cycle, 6–8, 52–53
accounts in general ledger, 24
accounts payable, 64–65
accounts payable ledger, 79
accounts receivable, 11
accounts receivable ledger, 79
accrual basis, 33–34, 82
accrued dividends payable, 38–39
accrued expenses adjustments, 38–39, 66–68
accrued investment income, 35–36
accuracy, 4
adjusted trial balance, 39, *41*
adjusting entries
   defined, 6, 34
   journalizing, 49
   overview, 34–39
   as step in accounting process, 7, 53
   on trial balance worksheet, 40–42
adjustments. *See* adjusting entries
American Institute of Certified Public Accountants, 13
analyzing transactions, 6, 52
asset accounts, 12, *23*. *See also* fixed assets

B

balance sheet
   examples, 15–16, *46*, *48*
   fixed assets on, 60
   formats, 46–49
   liability accounts on, 68–69
   overview, 12–14, 82
balance sheet accounts, on trial balance worksheet, 41–42
balance sheet equation, 15–17
bookkeeping, 5–8
books of original entry. *See* journals
buildings, common costs, 56
business owners, 3–4, 8–9
business types, 8–9

C

capital. *See* equity accounts
capital accounts, 13
cash basis, 33
cash disbursements journals, 77
cash receipts journals, 76–77
closing entries, 51–52, 53
closing the books, 7, 49–51, 82
common stock accounts, 13
computer-based accounting systems, 5–6, 81
computer depreciation, 60–61
consistency, 4–5
contingent liabilities, 64
contra accounts, 38, 60
control accounts, 78
corporations, 8–9, 13
cost of fixed assets, 56
creditors, 4
credits versus debits, 20–24
credit transactions, journals for, 74, *75*
credit unions
   business type, 9
   equity accounts of, 13–14
   subsidiary ledgers, 78
   types of transactions, 77
current liabilities, 68

D

debits and credits, 20–24
decision making, 3–4

INDEX

depreciation
  adjustments for, 37–38
  calculating, 56–58
  defined, 55
  examples, 60–61
  in subsidiary ledgers, 79
determinable liabilities, 63
directors, 3
double-entry accounting, 6, 17–18
double underline, 11

E

equipment, 56, 64–65. *See also* fixed assets
equity accounts
  accounting for, 71
  of credit unions, 13–14
  debits and credits, *23*
  overview, 12–13, 70
estimated liabilities, 63–64
expense accounts, closing, 50, 51, 71
expenses
  accrued, 38–39
  as cost, 56
  debits and credits, *23*
  defined, 11
explanation column, 24

F

financial stability, 4
financial statements
  balance sheet overview, 12–14
    (*see also* balance sheet)
  fixed assets on, 60–61
  income statement overview, 10–12
    (*see also* income statement)
  liability accounts on, 68–69
  order of presentation in, 39
  overview, 9–11
  preparing, 6, 45–49
  readiness for, 42
  as step in accounting process, 6, 53
fixed-asset ledgers, 79

fixed assets
  accounting for transactions, 59–60
  cost and service life, 56
  defined, 55
  depreciation, 37–38
  on financial statements, 60–61
formats
  of balance sheet and income statement, 10, 46, 49
  for journal entries, 20
furniture and equipment, 56, *75*. *See also* fixed assets

G

gain on sale, 61
general journal, 19, 24, 73
general ledger
  in accounting cycle, 6, 52, 53
  posting adjusting entries, 49
  subsidiary ledgers versus, 78
  transaction posting overview, 24–26, *30*
generally accepted accounting principles (GAAP), 4
government agencies, 4
grouping of accounts, 39

I

income
  on balance sheet, 16
  debits and credits, *23*
  defined, 11
income accounts, closing, 50, 51, 71
income statement
  defined, v
  examples, 17, *45*, *47*
  formats, 46
  overview, 10–12
  when to prepare, 45
income statement accounts, on trial balance worksheet, 41
income summary account, closing, 50, 51–52, 71
individual share and loan ledger, 78
insurance, prepaid, 36–37
investments, 15, 16, 35–36

J

journal and cash record, 77
journalizing, *7,* 49, 52
journals
   basic transaction recording, 6, 19–24, 49
   in computerized systems, 81
   entering fixed asset transactions, 59–60
   general ledger references, 25
   special, 74–77

L

land, inability to depreciate, 55
ledgers
   in accounting cycle, 6, 52, 53
   posting transactions to, 24–26, *30*
   subsidiary, 78–79, *80,* 81
liability accounts
   accounting for types, 64–68
   debits and credits, *23*
   defined, 63
   examples, 12
   shares as, 13
   types, 63–64
long-term liabilities, 68
losses, 61

M

management component of accounting, 5
manual accounting system overview, 6–8, 52–53
margin. *See* net income.
member shares. *See* shares

N

net income, 12
nominal accounts, 49–50
normal balance, 26, *30*
not-for-profit corporations, 9

O

"Other Accounts Credit" column, 76–77
owners, 3–4, 8–9

P

partnerships, 8, 13
payroll taxes, 65–66
periods benefited, 55
postclosing trial balance, 7, 52, 53
posting references
   in general ledger, 24–26, *30*
   in journals, 19, 20
posting transactions
   adjusting entries, 49
   overview, 24–26
   as step in accounting process, 6, 52, 53
prepaid expenses adjustments, 36–37
profit. *See* net income.
profit and loss statement. *See* income statement
Prompt Corrective Action regulation, 51
property tax adjustments, 67
purchases journals, 74, *75*

R

real accounts, 50
receivables, 11, 79
regular reserves
   calculating, 70
   defined, 14, 70
   transfers to, 52, 71
regulatory compliance, 4
rent, prepaid, 36
reports, timing, 5
reserves. *See* regular reserves
retained earnings. *See* undivided earnings
retained earnings accounts, 13
revenue. *See* income

S

salaries payable, 38
sales journals, 74, *75*
salvage value, 58, 60
service life, 56
shares
   in balance sheet equation, 15
   control account for, 78
   as equities versus liabilities, 13
single underscore, 11

sole proprietorships, 8
special journals, 74–77
stability, 4
statement of financial condition. *See* balance sheet
straight-line depreciation, 57–58
subsidiary ledgers, 78–79, *80*, 81
surplus. *See* net income.

T

T accounts, 21, 26
taxes, 4, 65–66
timeliness, 4
transaction registers, 81
transactions
    as debits or credits, 22–24
    entering in journals, 19–24
types, 77
trial balance
    adjusted, 39
    overview, 30–31
    as step in accounting process, 6, 7, 52
    unadjusted, 31, *34*
    worksheets, 39–42, *43*, 82

U

unadjusted trial balance, 31, *34*
undivided earnings
    on balance sheet, 49
    defined, 14, 70
    examples, 16–17
    terminology, *12*
    transferring net income to, 50

W

withholding payable amounts, 66
worksheets
    preparing financial statements from, 45–49
    as step in accounting process, 53
    trial balance, 39–42, *43*, 82

CUNA & Affiliates Order Form

To place an order or ask a question:

Call (800)356-8010, press 3
(or dial ext. 4157)
7:30 a.m. to 6:00 p.m.
Monday–Friday, CST
Local calls (608)231-4157
TTY phone (800)356-8030

Fax (608)231-1869

Mail the order form to:
CUNA Customer Service
P.O. Box 333
Madison, WI 53701-0333

E-mail customerservice@cuna.com

Ship to:

Credit union

Attention

Street address for shipping

City/State/Zip

Bill to:

Credit union

Attention   Title

Address

City/State/Zip

Phone   Ext. #

Fax

Payment method

☐ Credit unions in U.S.:
No need to prepay, we'll bill you for the total amount of your order.

☐ Individuals and International customers:
Must prepay in U.S. dollars.

Quantity	Stock Number	Description	Unit Price	Total

Subtotal: We'll calculate the freight and handling (plus sales tax if applicable).

Prices subject to change based on reprints and revisions.

Thank you for your order!